Youth, Gospel, Liberation

Second Edition

by **Michael Warren**

THE WORLD OF
DON BOSCO
MULTIMEDIA

Other Titles on Youth and Justice from
Don Bosco Multimedia:
Justice (Guides to Youth Ministry Series)
by Thomas Bright and John Roberto
Poverty (Do It Justice! Series)
by Thomas Bright
Human Rights (Do It Justice! Series)
by Thomas Bright and John Roberto
*Good Things are For Sharing: Stewardship As A Way of Life for
Children* (Workbook)
The Challenge of Catholic Youth Evangelization (1993 Document
from the National Federation of Catholic Youth Ministry, Inc.)

Acknowledgements
Grateful acknowledgement is made to reprint: "Youth and the Churches,"
published as "Youth and Religious Education," from *Changing Patterns
of Religious Education* edited by Marvin J. Taylor. Copyright © 1984 by
Abingdon Press. Used by permission. "Young People and the Nuclear
Threat" is from *Youth Without a Future?* edited by Baum and Coleman,
Concilium (October, 1985). "The Silence of Young People" was pub-
lished as "School as Zone of Liberation" was published as "High Schools
with a Difference" by *The Living Light.* "Youth Politicization:
Consciousness Plus Engagement" was published under the title "Youth
Politicization: A Proposal for Education within Youth Ministry" by
Religious Education Journal.
"At Peace, At Rest" by Joyce Carol Oates, reprinted by permission of
Louisiana State University Press from *Women Whose Lives Are Food,
Men Whose Lives Are Money* by Joyce Carol Oates. Copyright © 1978
by Joyce Carol Oates.

Youth, Gospel Liberation, 2nd Edition
© 1994 Michael Warren
All Rights Reserved
Typeset in ITC Korinna, and DTC Kauflinn Bold
Printed in the U.S.A.
Published by Don Bosco Multimedia, 475 North Ave.,
New Rochelle, NY 10802-0845
ISBN 0-89944-274-9
1 / 94   9 8 7 6 5 4 3 2 1

Contents

Foreword 1

Introduction 3

1. Youth and the Churches: A Historical Survey........................7

2. The Silence of Young People.................................... 18

3. Youth Politicization: Awareness Plus Action 34

4. Facing the Problem of Popular Culture 49

5. Zone of Liberation: School.. 62

6. The Teacher's Ministry of Liberation 73

7. Young People, Weapons, Violence—and Alternatives..............80

8. A Spirituality of Reversibility... 91

9. Critical Consciousness Toward Peacemaking.......................99

10. Youth and Social Justice: A Possible Combination? 106

11. Youth Weekends: Assessing the Recent Past 116

12. Youth Weekends: A Critical Look Forward...........................128

13. Culture, Religion, and Youth..143

For the members of the original Youth for Peace team:
Connie Loos, Maureen Murray, Brian Donahue-Lynch,
Mary Ann Donahue-Lynch,
Barry Levy, Nancy Flanagan, and Susan Farrell.

𝒻OREWORD

In many if not in most ages the Christian Church has blessed and defended the existing order. Only a minority of Christians has publicly expressed what the Bible calls the spirit of prophecy. Prophecy in the Bible refers to the utterance of God's word as judgement on culture and society and as promise of a truly human life beyond oppression. Jesus and his disciples stood in this prophetic tradition. They were critics of the dominant culture, secular and religious. They prayed that God's will be done on earth: they anticipated the coming of God's reign. The subversive message of Jesus has never completely faded from the Church's memory.

Over the last decades, under the influence of Third World Christians, the Churches have recovered the spirit of prophecy in their official social teaching. Echoing the Hebrew prophets, the Catholic bishops of the United States have this to say in their pastoral letter on economic justice: "For prophetic faith, to know the Lord means to do justice, and doing justice brings knowledge of the Lord. For this reason the prophets reject religious practices and rites which become a pretext for avoiding the demands of justice. Without justice, neither creed nor cult is of any avail.... To turn aside from those on the margins of society, the needy and the powerless, is to turn away from Jesus who identifies himself with them."

Contemporary ecclesiastical documents published by Latin American and North American bishops, seconded by recent Vatican teaching, present Jesus as the gracious liberator of humankind. We are told that the salvation that Jesus has brought includes the liberation of people from political, economic, and cultural oppression. Christian faith perceived in this way offers a critique of culture and society and summons the believers to struggle for the transformation of their world. A new technical phrase, "the preferential option for the poor," is used in these church documents to articulate the meaning of Christian discipleship in the present age.

While it is easy to spell out the general principles of the Church's new critical stance, it is very difficult to work out the meaning of the new perspective for the Church's pastoral ministry: the ministry to the local congregation, to children and young people, to the sick and the dying, to various classes and sectors of society. How can the Church communicate the new orientation?

In search of answers, Christian theologians have engaged in dialogue with secular philosophers and social scientists who also offer an ethical critique of society and clarify the contradictions of contemporary culture. The intellectual endeavor of these scholars is sometimes called Critical Theory. Out of commitment to human life beyond domination, social thinkers of various disciplines reflect critically on the world to which they belong, clarify the cultural symbols, economic structures, and political powers that cause oppression, and give new validity to liberating counter-trends of past and present that support the social movement for emancipation. The prolonged dialogue of theologians with this critical literature has resulted in a specifically Christian critical theology.

Michael Warren's *Youth, Gospel, Liberation* belongs to this new Christian literature. The author attempts what few Christian educators have dared to do: he seeks to apply the prophetic stance of Christian faith to the education of young people. It is no longer possible to propose a positive message to young people in the naive hope that they are ready to hear what is being said to them. What is required first is a critique of the prevailing culture and of the social conditions society has created for young people of different classes. It is necessary to uncover the myths and illusions in which society brings up young people to disguise from them the inequality, injustice, exploitation, and violence that characterize the present age. Faith is here first a critique of culture.

Only after the author has paid serious attention to the negative phase does he turn to the positive contribution the Christian religion is intended to make to the creation of a new, liberating social awareness. Can young people in our schools be taught to see themselves as responsible agents in society in solidarity with all who suffer injustice? Michael Warren trusts that the Christian message has this power. In conversation with authors of diverse disciplines and relying on his own experience as a teacher, the author has produced a book on the critical education of youth that is new and imaginative.

Gregory Baum

INTRODUCTION

This book comes out of a concern over the past decade or so to examine and understand the various influences shaping the consciousness and life structure of young people. I had touched on that matter somewhat in *Youth and the Future of the Church* (1982), especially in its most frequently cited chapter, "Youth Ministry: Towards Politicization." In the present work, I continue to examine the way young people are situated in the institutions of society: school, church, and communications structures. Here also I continue my concern with giving youth access to ways of understanding the workings of power in society and also lines of action in addressing or even "talking back" to social structures that can assume the unwitting compliance of young people in plans about which they have had no say.

An assumption underlying most of what is in these reflections is that youth are in a period of emerging commitments. Many agencies in our society recognize this fact, and so we should not be surprised that various agencies are encouraging young people to commit their life energies to various projects. I claim that religious persons have a right and a duty to judge these projects from a religious perspective, and, of course, Christians, from the perspective of discipleship to Jesus. Many who intervene in the lives of young people—including far too many in the churches—do so out of unexamined assumptions about young people that need to be challenged directly.

I fear that sometimes those working with youth do not step back enough from social structures to judge them in the light of the gospel. It is entirely too possible to hand on to young people the vision of the dominant culture, covered over with a religious veneer. To do so is infidelity, not just infidelity to a religious vision but infidelity to young people themselves. Those who hope to call youth to commitments worthy of a human life need to help them observe and judge, to apprise and appraise.

An underlying question discernible in every chapter of this work is: **How can we re-imagine the role of young people in the church and in society?**

This question must be asked in a time when young people, at every turn, find themselves imagined at their least: as greedy, lustful, violent, characterized by trivial concerns and narcissistic self-preoccupation. This is the image of youth we find in films, on TV, in music, and in advertisements everywhere. That imagination of young people is at fundamental odds with the imagination of human possibilities offered us by Jesus. More and more, I find the key gospel passage for young people to be the incident of the rich young man, for the way Jesus follows a step at a time the young man's sense of "more," summoning him to the most radical option open to him: solidarity with the poor and marginals. The young man does not elect, at least not at that moment, to follow that deepest call of Jesus, and indeed Jesus clearly says that God will be with him notwithstanding. The point is that Jesus saw in that young person the possibilities of bonding with his sisters and brothers in need—and of doing so as a way of being holy. *Jesus re-imagined his life for him,* but in ways quite counter to the imagination offered him by his socio-economic status.

My hope for this book is that it will be a factor in encouraging those in youth ministry similarly to re-imagine the lives of young people along the lines of Jesus' own imagination. Initially, the challenge of this book may seem to be one of finding enough time to finish it. Ultimately, however, the deeper and more enduring challenge, lasting far beyond the reading, will be to work with others to devise ways of being with young people that will open them to a deeper encounter with the Jesus we name Lord, to a critical understanding of the world we inhabit, and to commit their talents to fostering the common good. The challenge of this book is the challenge to re-think strategies of youth ministry that have become too comfortable or simply stale. This is not a challenge always to do something new but rather to find deeper, firmer foundations to our efforts.

If any characteristic binds all the chapters here, it may be that, as I suggested above, they all in one way or another strive to reconceptualize, in the sense that they seek to offer a gospel-based vision of youth in church, society, and culture. This is a vision that sees youth's contribution to all three areas, as not marginal but seminal and substantial. To highlight this feature of the book is to state clearly that I am trying to take a consistent stance toward youth and to elaborate a coherent laying out of that stance. At the same time, what I offer here is far from the final word on any of the topics I deal with. In fact, the very title I have selected, which leaves vague the precise relationship among "youth, gospel, and liberation," is meant to suggest that the precise relationship among these realities needs to be explored by many future writers, among whom I hope to take my place. This book is far from the last word.

Foreword to the Second Edition

The brief life of this book's original edition held many surprises for me. First, of its very many reviews the most serious were written by Protestant youth specialists and appeared in publications of Protestant denominations. Secondly, it is the only book I have written that sparked spontaneous phone calls from readers, who tracked me down to my home to let me know of their excitement at reading a work spelling out so many of their own hunches and intuitions about youth ministry. In every case these readers were also Protestants. Thirdly, considering the response it received, I hoped for a significant increase in writing about the social context and assumptions of ministry with youth. However, with the exception of some of the *Guides for Youth Ministry*, produced by the Center for Youth Ministry Development and published by Don Bosco Multimedia, and one or two other works, the increase in attention to the social and cultural aspects of youth has not yet materialized.

My hope is that the new, expanded paperback edition will make *Youth, Gospel, Liberation* available to many more persons and in many more countries than the first edition. An even deeper hope is new readers will find in it encouragement to trust their own vision and dare to write the new books needed to clarify the importance of liberation and justice in our ministry with the young. I have long been impressed with the ancient way Irish seanaches often ended a story: "That's my story. May the next to tell it better it." It is the blessing I send with this revised edition.

Jamaica, New York
September 1993

Chapter 1
Youth and the Churches:
A Historical Survey

This book re-examines some assumptions about young people and about the way social agencies should interact with them, particularly the social agency we call the church. Our assumptions tend to be hidden from us, but they may become clearer when we examine the way youth have been regarded in the history of various societies, particularly our own. If we ground our work in a better knowledge of that history, we may avoid much misunderstanding about what the possibilities of young people actually are, about what the appropriate social policies for dealing with youth may be, and about the position the churches should take in their work with youth.

This chapter offers an overview of attitudes and policies towards the religious side of young people in the United States, stressing the period after 1740. Surveying such a long period means treating briefly matters that merit considerable study; so I have documented my sources carefully to encourage such further study. Readers must also be warned that the history of religious groups in the United States is complex and that generalizations could lead to misunderstandings.[1] For instance, much of the following report reflects the experience of the better-documented denominational histories; it excludes such well-documented but not fully mainstream early histories as those of the Roman Catholic and Southern Baptist churches.

Early Attitudes Toward Religious Nurture

Before the gradual religious decline in the colonies that began around 1700, New England Congregationalism stressed the importance of a Christian upbringing in childhood. In general parents believed there was a covenant relationship between them and God that affected all members of a particular household.[2] These ideas changed, however, as a result of the Great Awakening of 1740-42, when religious fervor was rekindled by the preaching of revivalists such as Jonathan Edwards and George Whitefield.[3] Although the awakening fluctuated in intensity over the years, its effects can be traced right up to the outbreak of the Civil War. During these years, emphasis was placed on the dramatic and radi-

cal conversion which brought a person suddenly and decisively to salvation through Jesus. Though such a "turning" could occur anywhere
between childhood and adulthood, it was generally expected after puberty as one approached adulthood.[4]

This revivalist stress on conversion affected adult perceptions of
children, if not in every denomination, then at least in general. Christian
parentage notwithstanding, the child was seen to be a "child of wrath,"
under the domination of Satan. There was little expectation that the child
could engage in the intense struggle necessary before one could move
from Satan's ways to Christian discipleship. Children were allowed to
remain like fallow fields building up receptivity for the eventual planting.
As Luther Weigle describes the situation,

> [children] were held to be lost in sin, depraved by nature, and in need of
> a wholly new heart. They were children of wrath until the Holy Spirit
> should transmute them into children of God. It mattered nothing what
> their parentage, or what the quality of the home in which they were
> brought up....Older folk can do nothing for them, then, save to seek to
> deepen in them a sense of their need, and to pray on their behalf for the
> gift of conversion.[5]

Such attitudes show not so much an anti-child bias as a conviction
that the church was not meant to be a gathering of any and all who call
themselves Christians, but rather of a fervent elite.[6] Jonathan Edwards
and the others were offering a corrective, and a religiously elevated one,
to church life that had become halfhearted and half-committed.[7]
Ironically, the revival instigated by Jonathan Edwards, native of the
Hartford area and graduate of Yale, was later softened and, as far as its
treatment of children was concerned, corrected by Horace Bushnell, a
Yale graduate who spent his entire life as a pastor in Hartford.[8]

In 1847, Bushnell after struggling intellectually with the prevailing
practice of almost ignoring the religious development of children, published *Christian Nurture*, a work that set forth the theory and practice of
the Christian formation of children and young people. In what is often
quoted as the kernel of his position, Bushnell explained his conviction
that proper nurture would make it possible for

> the child to grow up a Christian, and never know himself [sic] as being
> otherwise. In other words, the aim, effort, and expectation should be,
> not, as is commonly assumed, that the child is to grow up in sin, to be
> converted after he comes to a mature age; but that he is to open on the
> world as one that is spiritually renewed, not remembering the time when
> he went through a technical experience, but seeming rather to have
> loved what is good from his earliest years.[9]

Throughout this book, Bushnell shows a keen sense of the importance of socialization in the development of children. Not only the family, but the local church community has a decisive impact, for better or worse, on the spirits of the young:

> But suppose there is really no trace or seed of holy principle in your children; has there been no fault of piety and constancy in your church? No want of Christian sensibility and love to God? No carnal spirit visible to them and to all, and imparting its noxious and poisonous quality to the Christian atmosphere in which they have had their nurture? For it is not for you alone to realize that this is included in the idea of Christian education. It belongs to the church of God, according to the degree of its social power over you and in you and around your children, to bear a part of the responsibility with you.[10]

These somewhat utopian convictions of Bushnell appear to have been decisive for the eventual and increasing preoccupation of the Protestant churches with careful intervention in the lives of children and youth. What Bushnell offered as a thesis in 1847 came to be the dominant agenda for young people in the majority of Protestant churches. Even the Sunday schools, which had been established in great numbers along with the Atlantic seaboard after the War of 1812 to instruct children of the poor in reading and writing, eventually became instruments devoted to Christian nurture; indeed, they became the key instruments.[11]

In the early republic (1790-1840), most children moved quickly from a brief period of dependency to a state of semi-dependence which was a jarring mixture of complete freedom and total subordination.[12] Many children ceased at an early age to be subject to complete parental control, even if only for a summer of labor on a neighboring farm.[13]

> Full incorporation [into the work force], moreover, probably occurred around the time of puberty—that is, at 15 or 16, when a boy was judged physically able to carry a man's work load. Prior to the middle of the 19th century, contemporaries associated puberty with rising power and energy rather than with the onset of an awkward and vulnerable stage of life which would later become known as adolescence....Since children entered the work force in stages, it is not surprising that contemporaries customarily distinguished infancy, boyhood, and young manhood. A second measure of passage out of infancy [was] the commencement of departure from home.[14]

A social system of apprenticeships, an acceptance of serious work for a child starting around age seven, and frequent orphanings, due to the early deaths of parents, all combined to set up myriad forms of semi-dependency for children.

The semi-independency of so many young people affected the kinds of associations they had among themselves. Especially in the large towns and cities of the early nineteenth century, young people gathered in voluntary associations which they organized and ran themselves. These included academies, a variety of young men's societies, and political clubs.[15] When all the members of a group were minors, they needed an adult sponsor for legal purposes. But the groups themselves tended to be independent rather than adult-dominated. The criteria for the attainment of adulthood were: entering marriage, leaving home for the last time, or in some cases the age at which one joined a church.

Evolution of Nurture as Control

After 1840, a number of social forces combined with the theory of Christian nurture to restrict, gradually but ineluctably, the independence of young people. One of these was the rise of the public school, begun earlier in Britain as a reform movement seeking to instill moral virtue via carefully managed schooling.[16] Another was the application of newly developed principles of organizational management to the creation of carefully engineered environments, such as orphan asylums and youth programs like the YMCA, to produce the internalization of moral restraint and the formation of character.[17] In addition, the conscious spacing of children led to a declining birth rate and to more attention to the task of child rearing.[18] Buttressed by economic forces, these philosophical and social factors combined to ensure that in the second half of the nineteenth century more and more of childhood and youth was spent in institutional settings intent upon the careful nurture, if not control, of young people, leading eventually to diminished opportunities for young people to direct their own activities. As Kett points out,

> the difference between the early and late nineteenth century lay not
> merely in the extension of ecclesiastical control over the spare-time
> activities of youth but in the increasing erosion of the principle of volun-
> tary association by youth. The young men's societies of the seventeenth
> through early nineteenth centuries had been organized by young men
> themselves; the young people's movement of the 1880s and 1890s, in
> contrast, consisted entirely of adult-sponsored youth organization.[19]

Christian nurture kept pace, becoming better organized, better staffed, and more carefully thought through—with results which, from our present standpoint at least, are open to question and critique. During the period 1880-1900, church youth organizations particularly felt the influence of "muscular Christianity," a concept imported from Britain that stressed planning, structure, and discipline in youth work. The "young people's movement" spawned by muscular Christianity affected millions of Protestant youth at the end of the nineteenth century, "far more young people than did public high schools." [20]

Unfortunately, using the rhetoric of nurture, many of these efforts were intended to protect young people from "moral dangers," to shield them from reality and to some extent from adult questions and tasks. Sincerity was more significant than competence, predictability more important than probing inquiry. "Even when spokesmen for the young people's movement outlined specific goals, they were so general as to be meaningless...or so trivial as to be ludicrous."[21] In sum,

> for all the talk about activity...the motive force behind church youth soci-
> eties in the 1880s and 1890s was defensive, a desire to shield young
> people from contamination by the alien culture of big cities and immi-
> grants...A common thread which ran through college "life," the high
> school extra-curriculum, and Christian youth organizations was hostility
> to precocity, to adult behavior in youth. As it acquired institutional
> forms, the long-standing fear of precocity changed its shape. The avoid-
> ance of precocity no longer entailed merely the removal of intellectual
> pressures and social stimulants from youth, but the creation of a self-
> contained world in which prolonged immaturity could sustain itself.[22]

The irony in these programs was that the questions and activities of youth all tended to be set by adults who at the same time seemed to be shielding youth from adult questions and adult activities. In these settings religious nurture tended toward passivity and insularity.[23]

The move in church youth work toward adult domination of youth activities continued into the twentieth century, and even increased as part of a wider societal program of exercising more and more control over the lives of young people. In part, the progress of these programs was itself tied to a growing move toward professionalization in the United States. Standards were set for training and performance, and professionals were expected to have greater technical control over the tasks they performed. Adult domination and professionalization both coalesced in the first quarter of the twentieth century in the transformation of the Sunday school from a nurture-centered to an education-centered activity.

The Shift from Nurture to Education

The shift was engineered by a cadre of thinkers influenced by the progressive educational theories of John Dewey and by the relatively short-lived social gospel theology of Walter Rauschenbusch.[24] The desire of these professionals was to shift the emphasis of the church school from informal procedures and educationally haphazard materials to a professional combination of the best thinking about education and about religion. In a new century ready to move away from the unenlightened practices of the past, the religious education professionals judged that the Sunday school should become a respectable educational institution. The efforts of these reformers were greatly assisted by the formation in 1903 of the Religious Education Association. Founded by William Rainey Harper as an organization free of any sort of ecclesiastical control, the association was to be an umbrella organization for all those concerned with promoting religious and moral education.[25] At its 1905 convention, the REA set forth its ideal of fostering a proper conjunction of education and religion: "To inspire the educational forces of our country with the religious ideal; to inspire the religious forces of our country with the educational ideal; and to keep before the public mind the ideal of religious education and the sense of its need and value."[26]

One of the chief theorists of the new religion-and-education thrust was George Albert Coe, professor at Union Theological Seminary, a radical and progressive on every front: political, educational, and theological.[27] Coe was imbued with an intense faith in the human potential as it seemed to be emerging in the early years of the century. Such was his faith in the future that "few of his students [were] encouraged to study history; instead their attention [was] focused upon the present and the ongoing struggle of freeing men from the burden of a dead past."[28]

Coe and other leaders of the religious education movement succeeded for almost thirty years in professionalizing the education structures that had evolved in the churches:

> [They] looked upon this hustle and bustle [of the average Sunday school] as empty efforts of well-intentioned workers, amateurs who had too long dominated the Sunday school. Amateurism was, in fact, the nub of their quarrel with the traditional movements. Professional leadership must take over. Any why not? Experts were evident in public schools, social work and municipal life. Should Protestant education be different? Volunteer leaders, in the reformers' scheme, should be aided by a fulltime "director of religious education" if a congregation could afford one. If not, the minister was expected to assume the mantle of the professional....The formula was straightforward: no professional, no reform; no reform, no school worthy of respect.[29]

Although not all those leading the religious education movement walked in lockstep with each other,[30] in general the effort to professionalize the educational side of religious education went unquestioned for thirty years, as did the effort to open the religious side to intellectual inquiry. These reformers, however, succeeded more at the theoretical level than at the level of local church practice.

In local churches religious education depended on the efforts of many volunteer laypersons, at least some of whom cherished their memories of the good old days of the non-professionalized Sunday school. In rural areas the optimistic and rationalistic faith of the new professionals was coolly received. In both urban and rural settings, some volunteers found that "the methods of progressive education—the experience-centered approach with stress on problem-solving and attention to students' needs—required a sophistication and commitment of time" not feasible for them.[31] And then, of course, in many places the life of the local Sunday school had gone on as if there never had been a religious education movement.

Eventually, the social optimism of what was called liberal theology was dealt a lethal blow by World War I, before collapsing entirely in the pessimism accompanying the economic collapse of 1929.[32] More and more through the 1930s, voices were raised to question religious education, particularly its adequacy as a vehicle for religious faith. Finally, in 1941, H. Shelton Smith wrote his *Faith and Nurture*, a book decisive for moving the question away from the fixities of the early religious education movement and back to a quest for the appropriate context for the development of religious faith.[33] In the forty years since Smith's attempt to critique the religious education movement, especially the Coe-Childs wing of it, the literature of religious education and Christian education has hovered between the poles of education and nurture.

Thinking About the Nurture of Faith

A substantial amount of writing has attempted to shed light on various aspects of the question in the decades since 1941, and it would be impossible here to treat even a small fraction of this literature. What is significant is that the question itself remains unresolved. Some people contend that the whole field of religious education is in confusion; others find in the ongoing discussion an enriching vitality that refuses to offer or accept simplistic answers to complex questions. Indeed, there have been many attempts at synthesis, to avoid what is seen as a false choice between education and the nurture of faith. Because of its special relevance for youth ministry theory, the writer wishes to turn to one stream of this literature, the one that pays special attention to socialization theory.

Since about 1965, when C. Ellis Nelson gave the Sprunt lectures at Union Theological Seminary in Richmond, Virginia, later published as *Where Faith Begins*, some writers have sought to combine education and the nurture of faith through a nurturing community.[34] These thinkers ask if the life of the community could be centered in the scrutiny of con-

temporary culture in the light of religious meaning. Such thinking does
not look to instructional strategies to communicate religious traditions,
nor to activities for children organized and dominated by adults. Without
rejecting their value, these thinkers prefer to examine interaction among
community members and the many informal ways they influence each
other. The main contention of *Where Faith Begins* is "that religion at its
deepest levels is located within a person's sentiments and is the result of
the way he [sic] was socialized by the adults who cared for him as a
child."[35] Nelson's thesis "is that faith is communicated by a community of
believers and that the meaning of faith is developed by its members out
of their history, by their interaction with each other, and in relation to the
events that take place in their lives."[36] The community's buildings and
budget, its worship, its way of dealing or not dealing with conflict, its
forms of leadership are all ways of communicating its core meanings.
However, everything needs to be put under the scrutiny of Scripture and
a quest for discipleship appropriate to the current age.

    This attention to religious socialization among Protestants has cre-
ated new possibilities for dialogue and mutual enrichment with Roman
Catholics, whose own catechetical renewal has an emphasis on socialization. John Westerhoff's *Will Our Children Have Faith?*[37] finds a wide
audience among Roman Catholics, while Westerhoff acknowledges his
own debt to catechetical theory.[38] Catechetical theory holds that "catechesis in the final analysis is community education. The community of faith
with all its formal and informal structures is the chief catechist."[39]
However, for catechesis to be effective, the community itself needs to
undergo continuous conversion, broadening its horizons, reforming and
renewing itself, through an ongoing process of interpreting and reinter-
preting its response to the gospel.

    In Roman Catholic understanding, catechesis falls within the cate-
gory of ministry rather than education.[40] Without in any way ignoring
education or educational theory, catechesis finds the more appropriate
frame of reference for its activities within ministry, leading to a renewed
understanding of youth ministry and thus of youth nurture. To be effective, ministry with youth must attend to the multiple needs of youth, bal-
ancing the ministries of the Word, of worship, of guidance and counsel
(including education), and of healing. The ministry of the Word encom-
passes all those activities by which the church maintains and proclaims
the meanings that bind it together. The ministry of worship is the activity
by which a community embodies its understandings and its group life.
The ministry of guidance and counsel, including education, embodies
those activities by which a community comforts the troubled, shares its
wisdom about the human condition, and liberates the human spirit. The
ministry of healing involves those activities by which a community fol-

lows Jesus' mandate to free the captives, feed the hungry, bind up the wounded, and be a force for justice.[41]

Seen from this angle, youth ministry operates out of the community's life. As a nurturing activity, youth ministry is not content with summoning young people to an intense and warm fellow-feeling within a peer group. Important as such intense experiences seem to be for young people, a properly nuanced ministry with youth pays attention to the distance between much in current culture and the norms of human life set forth in the gospel. When seeking to critique culture, youth ministry is more about challenge than about comfort.

The best youth ministry thinking of recent years has stressed the need for a strong intellectual and educational component, worked out through innovative strategies. Considering the manipulation of the consciousness of youth in an electronic culture and the difficulty of developing the political awareness of young people, education will have to receive increasing attention in the future. Similarly, as works such as Kett's become more widely known, those working for youth nurture through youth ministry will need to guard against offering young people domesticating strategies and trivial ideas. Youth ministry seems headed for a period of creative dissatisfaction with its own achievements and agenda. Out of these directions we may hope that the churches will find their way to be ever more faithful to their young people.

---

[1]Robert W. Lynn offers several such warnings in a fine article that has been of special help in preparing this survey. See Robert W. Lynn, "The Uses of History: An Inquiry into the History of American Religious Education," *Religious Education* 67, no. 2 (March-April 1972): 83-97. Also, Anne Boylan, *Sunday School: The Formation of an American Institution 1790-1880* (Yale University Press, 1988), esp. Chapter 9: "Conversion and Christian Nurture," pp. 133-165.

[2]Williston Walker, "Horace Bushnell," in Horace Bushnell, *Christian Nurture* (New Haven: Yale University Press, 1967), p. xxviii. Actually the situation seems to have been somewhat more complex than Walker's description of it. Even children from thoroughly Christian homes were expected eventually to undergo a conversion in adulthood. See Sydney E. Ahlstrom, *A Religious History of the American People* (New Haven: Yale University Press, 1972), pp. 141-163. See also *Theology in America*, ed. Sydney E. Ahlstrom (New York: bobbs-Merrill, 1967), pp. 26-36, especially p. 34, n. 12.

[3]Luther Weigle, "Introduction," in Bushnell, *Christian Nurture*, pp. xxxii-xxxiii.

[4]Although conversion was to come close to adulthood, it is important to realize it was prepared for in early years. Joseph Kett notes "the fact that in religious households piety was to begin early. Conversion in youth was often the outcome of a process that commenced at 7 or 8, with the symptoms going into remission in ensuing years." Joseph F. Kett, *Rites of Passage: Adolescence in America, 1790 to the*

Present (New York: Basic Books, 1977), p. 68. The Shaker communities welcomed children to live among them and gave them a careful formation until maturity (age 14 for girls, 16 for boys), when they had to make a decision either to leave and grow toward conversion in the "world" or to remain through the making of a formal commitment. See Edward Deming Andrews, *The People Called Shakers* (New York: Dover, 1963), pp. 186-94.

[5]Weigle, in *Christian Nurture*, p. xxxiii.

[6]Ahlstrom, *Theology in America*, pp. 33-34.

7See Walker in *Christian Nurture*, p. xxix, and Ahlstrom, *Theology in America*, pp. 34-35.

[8]For a vivid account of the thought about conversion prior to Bushnell, see Kett, *Rites of Passage*, pp. 63-68. It is important for readers to note that Kett's book focuses on the history of males, because of the scant documentation about women.

[9]Bushnell, *Christian Nurture*, p. 4.

[10]Ibid., 5-6.

[11]Kett, *Rites of Passage*, p. 120. Kett's focus is males in adolescence.

[12]Ibid., p. 29.

[13]Ibid., pp. 15-30 for a detailed treatment of childhood during this period, 1790-1840.

[14]Ibid., p. 17.

[15]Ibid., pp. 30-31 and pp. 38-41.

[16]See ibid., pp. 111-15. See also pp. 186-89 for a treatment of more technical bureaucratic controls in schools at a later point in history.

[17]See David H. Rothman, *The Discovery of the Asylum: Social Order and Disorder in the New Republic* (Boston: Little, Brown and Co., 1971), esp. pp. 206-36.

[18]Kett, *Rites of Passage*, pp. 112-25.

[19]Ibid., p. 194.

[20]Ibid., p. 190.

[21]Ibid., p. 194.

[22]Ibid., p. 210.

[23]A suggestion of the insularity of the Sunday school can be found in Mark Twain's depiction of Tom Sawyer's Sunday school superintendent, who "was very earnest of mien, and very sincere and honest of heart; and he held sacred things and places in such reverence, and so separated them from worldly matters, that unconsciously to himself his Sunday-school voice had acquired a peculiar intonation which was wholly absent on weekdays." Cited Robert W. Lynn and Elliott Wright, *The Big Little School* (New York: Harper & Row, 1971), p. 75.

[24]Ibid., p. 80. See also pp. 75-85.

[25]In the beginning the REA was not intended to be a professional organization but to bring together professionals and laypersons to foster communication. See Boardman W. Kathan, "Report," *Reach* 11, no. 1 (Spring 1981): 2.

[26]"The Aims of Religious Education," in *Proceedings of the Third Annual Con-*

vention of the Religious Education Association (Chicago: Religious Education Association, 1905), p. 474. For a good description of William Rainey Harper's desire to professionalize church education, see Boardman W. Kathan, "William Rainey Harper: Founder of the Religious Education Association," *Religious Education* 73, no. 5S (September-October 1978): S7-S16.

[27]See Helen A. Archibald, "George A. Coe: The Years from 1920-1951," *Religious Education* 73, no. 5S (September-October 1978): S25-S35.

[28]Lynn, "Uses of History," p. 87.

[29]Lynn and Wright, *Big Little School,* p. 83.

[30]See Lynn, "The Uses of History," pp. 86-87

[31]Lynn and Wright, *Big Little School*, p. 85.

[32]A detailed account of this inflated social optimism and the gloom that followed in its wake can be found in Russell B. Nye, *This Almost Chosen People* (Ann Arbor: Michigan State University Press, 1966), pp. 1-41. George A. Coe's social optimism can be revisited in his work, *A Social Theory of Religious Education* (New York: Charles Scribner's Sons, 1917).

[33]A valuable account of this period can be found in Kieran Scott, "Religious Education and Professional Religious Education: A Conflict of Interest?" *Religious Education* 78, no. 5 (January-February 1983).

[34]C. Ellis Nelson, Where Faith Begins (Richmond, Va: John Knox, 1967). See also, Nelson's more recent, *How Faith Matures* (Louisville: John Knox, 1989).

[35]Ibid., p. 9.

[36]Ibid., p. 10.

[37]John H. Westerhoff III, *Will Our Children Have Faith?* (New York: Seabury, 1976). See also his essay, "Fashioning Christians in Our Day," pp. 262-281, of Stanley Hauerwas and John H. Westerhoff, *Schooling Christians* (Grand Rapids: Eerdmans, 1992).

[38]John H. Westerhoff III, "A Call to Catechesis," *The Living Light* 14, no. 3 (1977): 354-58. See also "Catechesis: An Anglican Perspective," in *Sourcebook for Modern Catechetics*, ed. Michael Warren (Winona, Minn.: St. Mary's 1983).

[39]Berard Marthaler, "Socialization as a Model for Catechetics," in *Foundations of Religious Education*, ed. Padraic O'Hare (New York: Paulist, 1978), pp. 64-92, especially p. 89.

[40]See "Schools, Education, and Catechesis," Chapter 1 of Michael Warren, *Faith, Culture and the Worshiping Community* (Washington, DC: Pastoral Press, 1993), pp. 1-22.

[41]See Michael Warren, "Youth Ministry: Toward Politicization," Chapter 9 of *Youth and the Future of the Church* (New York: Seabury, 1982), pp. 89-102.

Chapter 2
The Silence of Young People

An important feature of contemporary church work with youth consists in replacing the nineteenth century legacy, of programs limited to trivial concerns—programs which offered them a largely privatized view of their own lives and extended their dependence on adults. So persistent and taken-for-granted is this legacy that many have difficulty seeing it. Here I wish to examine a single feature of this legacy that tends to characterize youth in our time: silence. The silence of young people in our society is not only a fact but a problem. Many readers will dispute it, quickly pointing out the tendency toward loud speech and highly expressive gestures among young people, especially when in groups. Parents may protest vigorously that, far from being a problem, the silence of young people is exactly what they yearn for, even brief interludes of silence.

However, when I speak of the silence of young people, I am referring to their capacity for a public life. What I have in mind is akin to the kind of silence Tillie Olsen writes of in her book, *Silences*. The silences she explores are those of women in literary history, the silence of women who have not been able to articulate in writing their experience of life. She writes:

> Literary history and the present are dark with silences: some [are] the silences for years by our acknowledged great; some silences hidden; some the ceasing to publish after one work appears; some the never coming to book form at all.

> These are not natural silences, that necessary time for renewal, lying fallow, gestation, in the natural cycle of creation. The silences I speak of here are unnatural; the unnatural thwarting of what struggles to come into being but cannot.[1]

Olsen believes that "compared to the countless centuries of the silence of women, compared to the century preceding ours—the first in which women wrote in any noticeable numbers—ours has been a favorable one."[2] And yet in our own century, there has been only one woman writer of achievement for every twelve distinguished male writers. In the 19th and early 20th centuries, almost all women writers of distinction were unmarried or married late in their thirties.[3] In our century almost all literary achievement among women has come from childless women.[4]

Through her own literary gifts, Olsen is able to uncover for us the diminishment of the human race hidden in these facts. We can get some glimpse of what we have lost by studying the contributions of those few women who did move from silence to public articulation of their experience, including those who wrote under male pseudonyms. Olsen also uncovers the social presuppositions about women and the social condition of women that imposed the deafening silence she describes. In a sense Olsen's book is a book of mourning for the suppressed human revelation and the lost art of all the women who had the talent to write but never did. Tillie Olsen is not alone in her mourning. Elizabeth Fiorenza in her book, *In Memory of Her*, similarly mourns the silence of women in the New Testament. Claiming that "androcentric Western language and patriarchal religion have `erased' women from history and made them `non-beings.'"[5] Fiorenza searches out the voices of women in the early church and recovers them for us, so that we can celebrate them.

Paulo Freire has dealt with a similar kind of silence. He has described how whole populations can be imprisoned in a "culture of silence" by structures clearly meant to keep them inarticulate. In Freire's description, power elites treat the masses as an object and do not expect to hear any original or articulate word from them. Even further, these elites try to control the very naming of the world in a way that abolishes any language that might expose the true situation of oppression. If the popular masses seem about to break their submissive silence, the power elites use whatever means they can to suppress such attempts, including violence.[6] Thus the undeniable task of such oppressed silence ones is to claim and then achieve their right to a voice, the right to pronounce their word. Being denied a voice is what Gustavo Gutierrez calls "cultural death," the taking away of all those things that give unity and strength to the dispossessed of the world.[7]

The Mute Ones

Are any of these reflections applicable to young people in our society? Do we find among youth a silence marking their inability to articulate their experience of life, either in individual literary accounts or through some sort of group voice? Is our society diminished by this silence? Is this silence reversible? I answer yes to all these questions but at the same time realize that many people, including some who work with youth, fail to see the significance of the issue. Let me suggest that significance.

Young people in our society are not only silent. They are a step beyond silence: they are mute. It is almost as if they have no significant life experience of which they themselves can speak. It is only later as older adults that they are able to look back and speak of the earlier period, the period of silence, the period of systematic inarticulateness. Even these later accounts are few. Most young people, it is sad to say, are never able to speak about their earlier experience.

I wish to highlight the fact that very few young people are ever encouraged to take their life experience seriously enough to want to articulate it. Let me apply to youth what Tillie Olsen says about writing and why it was that so many women did not attempt to write.

> How much it takes to become a writer. Bent (far more common than we assume), circumstances, time, development of craft—beyond that: how much conviction as to the importance of what one has to say one's right to say it. And the will, the measureless store of belief in oneself to be able to come to cleave to, find the form for one's own life comprehensions. Difficult for any male not born into a class that breeds such confidence. Almost impossible for a girl, a woman.[8]

What is the significance of a lack of conviction about what one has to say and of one's right to say it? What is the significance of such a lack of belief in oneself that it denies the self a chance to give form to one's "life comprehensions"? These questions help uncover for us the potential significance of the silence of young people.

There is an exception to the written silence of young people: the original depictions of their own lives which they write for the literary magazines published each year by most high schools and colleges. Here one can find original and valuable (although perhaps highly edited) depictions of prose, poetry, and art of what it is like to be young today. What the young reveal here about themselves is impressive, in sometimes quite artistic ways. These sources, however, receive scant public attention. As Rod Stewart wrote in an otherwise deplorable song: "There ain't no point in talking when there's nobody listening."[9] Because they are not taken seriously, these articulations remain quasi-private.

There is another dimension to the silence of youth that we must attend to. I refer to the lack of a group public voice for youth. The following example illustrates what I mean. Richard Rodriguez, in his autobiography *Hungry of Memory*, writes of working one college summer as a laborer with a group of Mexican aliens. By the end of the summer, toughened by physical labor and exposure to the sun, he was virtually indistinguishable from his Mexican fellow-workers, except for one important difference. "I was not one of *los pobres*," he writes. "What made me different from them was an attitude of mind, my imagination of myself." He goes on to explain that were he to work in a factory as his Mexican immigrant father had done, the experience would be different for him than it had been for his father. "My long education would favor me. I could act as a public person—able to defend my interests, my unionize, to petition, to speak up—to challenge and demand." Finally, he reflects on the parting from his Mexican *compadres* at the end of the summer:

> Their silence stays with me now. The wages those Mexicans received for their labor were only a measure of their disadvantaged condition. Their silence is more telling. They lack a public identity. They remain profoundly alien. Persons apart. People lacking a union obviously, people without grounds. They depend upon the relative good will or fairness of their employers each day.[10]

These words suggest for me something of what silence as the lack of a public voice means, even though I do not claim as Rodriguez seems to, that a long education is required for one to come to act as a public person.

The public group silence of young people in our country is a very serious matter. We live in a time where more and more young people openly question whether there will be a future.[11] Some young women question whether they should aspire to have children when they see every indication that these children might perish in a nuclear holocaust. Others, young women and men both, question whether any planning for such a precarious future is possible.[12] Such questions about the future are unprecedented in any period of human history and are among the most important questions of our time. What I have found so very curious is the inability of youth to come to public expression of these issues so much on their minds and so much at the heart of their own interests.

Could it be that in the U.S., our young people are afflicted with a fund of constriction, similar to that imposed on women writers? Tillie Olsen noted that for a long time women writing under their own names had not been allowed to write of the full range of human experience.[13] They were expected to write only of womanly matters, limiting their subjects to the sphere of the home. Are there similar socially imposed constrictions of the vision of young people? Are there matters young people are expected to pay attention to that in effect distract their attention from the matters on which they need to find a public voice? Do society's institutions have agenda for youth which in effect push out of sight matters of much more consequence?

School sports and school spirit are examples of trivializing matters which are proposed as worthy of intense energy and attention, but which result only in a pseudo-voice, as symbolized in the pre-packaged unison cheers led by well-prepared cheerleaders for the benefit of the team on the playing field.[14] These exercises use up attention and energy better focused on questions of greater significance, such as, understanding and prizing the common good and common welfare; concern for human communication, including relations among nations based on trust; and the possibility of asking what one's long-term contribution will be to the human community. Some might claim that youth are not concerned about such matters. My question is: What would happen if some of the energy we expend in calling youth's attention to more trivial, constricted matters was used to help them attend to these larger questions?

The lack of a public voice for youth could also be called a political silence. Young people assume that they in fact can have no significant impact on the world. The centers of power are inaccessible; the wielders of power are anonymous persons in these centers; the issues relating to power are so complex as to be incomprehensible. These assumptions lead to political silence, a conviction that one has nothing to say about the issues of one's time. Such assumptions keep youth from forming associations that could allow them to have a voice about matters affecting their own futures. Instead, their group voice tends to be limited to cheering at a sports event.

These questions about the silence of youth, in their personal articulation of their life experience and in their lack of a public voice, are not simple ones to answer. They are ultimately about social policy affecting youth, in the broadest sense of that policy, and any solution will have to involve shifts in social policy at all levels. But the complexity of this social policy must not hinder us from bringing to conscious and critical view the role of young people in our society. In the background lurk other complex questions about how schools are run and even about how we understand and teach literacy, questions about the way religious institutions deal with young people, and about the ideals of citizenship we offer them. All these questions need to be asked in searching ways by those committed to young people in our day.

The silence of youth is related to the matter of violence among young people. There is evidence that violence among teens has reached epidemic proportions in our day, and the epidemic cuts through all economic classes.[15] What is important to note is the way the violence is tied to youth's silence.[16] Many thinkers have dealt with the connection between the two, but the following assessment by Thomas Merton will suffice.

> Violence is essentially wordless, and it can begin only where thought and rational communication have broken down. Any society which is geared for violent action is by that very fact systematically unreasonable and inarticulate. Thought is not encouraged, and the exchange of ideas is eschewed as filled with all manner of risk. Words are kept at a minimum, at least as far as their variety and content may be concerned, though

they may pour over the armed multitude in cataracts; they are simply organized and inarticulate noise destined to arrest thought and release violence, inhibiting all desire to communicate with the enemy in any other way than by destructive impact.[17]

At some level the violence of young people is the frustrated surging of their voices, the way Billy Budd's death-dealing punch to Claggett was a way of saying with his fist what he could not say with his tongue. At some level also, disrupting the silence of youth may also break a pattern of violence among them.

Can it be done? Is it possible for those committed to the young to assist them toward self-expression, without taking on the entire question of social policy affecting youth? We may at least begin to do so if we engage them in three strategies: helping them re-name reality; helping them question the metaphors by which they are invited to interpret reality; and helping them find forms of public action.

Assistance in Re-Naming

In *Our Blood*, feminist Andrea Dworkin says that for women "one fundamental revolutionary act is to reclaim the power of naming, to define for ourselves what our experience is and has been."[18] Why should she make such a claim for naming? The answer, spelled out in complex ways in Dworkin's own book, has been best explained for me by the literary critic, George Steiner. Steiner asks how the murderous and even bestial falsehoods that propped up National Socialism in Nazi Germany could have succeeded? His answer is that it was propped up by language that either masked the horrors or shaped the consciousness of those who allowed them to occur.

Steiner reminds us that these horrors were perpetrated by people using human speech, and were ordered and defended in written documents using human language. Something must have happened to language when the unspeakable found its way into everyday discourse as if it were a matter of business as usual. If human speech is our first defense against the bestial, then when perverted, it becomes bestiality's first defense.[19]

Steiner claims that a human literacy can and must reaffirm its authority against jargon. He writes,

> In our time, the language of politics has become infected with obscurity and madness. No lie is too gross for strenuous expression, no cruelty too abject to find apologia in the verbiage of historicism. Unless we can restore to the words in our newspapers, laws, and political acts some measure of clarity and stringency of meaning, our lives will draw yet

nearer to chaos. There will then come to pass a new Dark Ages. The prospect is not remote.[20]

Steiner's case in point is the decline of the German language prior to Nazi era, a decline that prepared the way for the horrors under Hitler. It became infected with dead metaphors, stock similes, slogans. Words grew longer, ponderous, ambiguous. Jargon replaced precise common usage. The German people developed "a terrible weakness for slogans and pompous cliches; and automatic reverence before the long word or the loud voice; a fatal taste for saccharine pathos beneath which to conceal any amount of rawness or deception."[21] Steiner's account of success of this strategy is so chilling and yet so suggests the power of naming that I cite a long passage.

> The unspeakable [was] being said, over and over, for twelve years. The unthinkable being written down, indexed, filed for reference. The men who poured quicklime down the openings of the sewers in Warsaw to kill the living and stifle the stink of the dead wrote home about it. They spoke of having to "liquidate vermin." In letters asking for family snapshots or sending season's greetings. Silent night, holy night, Gemütlichkeit. A language being used to run hell, getting the habits of hell into its syntax. Being used to destroy what there is in man of man and to restore to governance what there is of beast. Gradually words lost their original meaning and acquired nightmarish definitions. Jude, Pole, Russe came to mean two-legged lice, putrid vermin which good Aryans must squash, as a party manual said, "like roaches on a dirty wall." "Final solution" came to signify the death of six million human beings in gas ovens. The language was infected not only with these great bestialities. It was called upon to enforce innumerable falsehoods, to persuade the Germans that the war was just and everywhere victorious...The language was turned upside down to say "light" where there was darkness.[22]

The distortions Steiner describes are exponentially increased in our own time in various parts of the globe because of the multiple agencies seeking to turn language to their own ends.[23] The advertising industry's ways of distorting language are so obvious that I will not deal with them here. The abuse of language by elected officials has been so serious in our own country that the word politician itself may now have subtle connotations of liar. One of the reasons so many laughed when Richard Nixon announced on national television just before leaving the White House, "I am not a crook," was that he had so obviously lied (the term he used for lying was stonewalling) so often, that this particular lie seemed incongruously funny.

However, perhaps the supreme distorter of language is the military, because of its need to rename for us the unspeakable.[24] Thus the MX missile, capable of killing 100 million persons is called the *peacekeeper*. In 1984 on the anniversary of the Normandy invasion, Army Secretary, John Marsh, unveiled a monument to U.S. soldiers killed on D-Day at Utah Beach. March said the monument was "not simply a tribute to the dead but to youth who did not grow old."[25] Such distorted language was also used in naming as heroes rather than as victims the Marines killed in their sleep in Lebanon, in a war even their leaders now admit they still do not understand. Little of this language-as-falsehood is new to those familiar with George Orwell's prophetic novel *1984*, with its unforgettable slogan "War is peace."

In such a situation of massive language distortion, what are the possibilities for those working with youth to aid them in embracing a language skeptical of doubletalk and able to expose debasing and destructive language? Will we be able to help them do what the women of Greenham Common in England did in exposing the falsity of the peace language used by the war-makers? "Here at Greenham Common," one of these women said, "where they are installing these new missiles, they are building the equivalent of the ovens and the trains for the next Holocaust." She was using language that unveils, language that counters the claims of those who insist that weapons make the peace.

It is possible to help young people learn to find the language for a proper re-naming of the world. However, it will not be done without helping them at the same time see through the false naming that seeks to mask evil. Perhaps before youth can be so helped, adults working with young people may themselves need to become more astute in naming reality. Perhaps many need to increase their skills in speaking to such distortions. For example, in October 1982, in Columbus, Ohio, Ronald Reagan described the nuclear freeze movement as inspired "not by the sincere, honest people who want peace, but by some who want the weakening of America."[26] Thus, if there are sincere and honest people working in the freeze movement, they are dupes of their freeze leaders, who are trying to subvert their own country. In this logic, to be for the freeze is to be unpatriotic and to be either lacking in integrity or a dupe of those lacking in integrity.

The problem in facing such distortions is not just one of talking back but of identifying the insinuations and distortions in such accusations and exposing them. Acquiring such a skill takes practice, and young people may need exercises involving the analysis of such distorted language. Such exercises could help young people become better attuned to all the language they encounter and help them actively contradict such naming of the work as is being done for them so facilely by the advertising and entertainment industries.

The matter of naming is even more complex than acquiring a skill at exposing distortion. One also needs a stance from which to name. When naming fits one's view of reality, one's stance, a person simply does not want to question the naming. What stance is appropriate for young people? One that is concerned with the future of the race and one that is based on the gospel. Possibly the most radical stance one could adopt is that of solidarity with victims. It is the stance Jesus himself took in proclaiming the reign of God that would correct injustice. However we phrase it, a proper stance would be toward the future, toward sisterhood and brotherhood among peoples, toward compassion and toward justice. Not all will want to adopt such a stance, but all could benefit by knowing that there is such a stance, that some espouse it, and that the espousing of it makes a difference in the way one looks at and lives one's life.

Young people today know or at least suspect something is radically wrong in the world. Their nightmares of the bright burning light that flashes cold death on the world, may be the seeds for a radical questioning of our time. Young people know something is crazy when nations have amassed a million times the destructive power of Hiroshima, when they could have been exploding one Hiroshima—sized blast every day since August 1945 and could go on doing so for centuries before exhausting their supply. Young people's sense that something is wrong could be the basis for tapping their spiritual energies toward compassion and human unity. For these energies to be tapped in a coherent and intelligent manner, young people need accurate information about the issues, tied to affirmation of their right to speak to these issues. Getting that information and developing a competent mastery of it is an educational task, though partly a task of self-education. In speaking of re-naming we cannot overlook the power that systematic and coherent accounts of reality have for the entire project of naming.

Assistance in Questioning Metaphors

A second strategy involves helping young people understand and then question the dominant metaphors of our society. Although our culture bombards us with images, the problem is that we look at reality through images.[27] Certain images provide the lenses through which we view reality. We are unaware of the lens because we are so busy looking through it. A good example of a mental image serving as a lens might be the image of woman in our society.[28] This image does not refer to any particular woman or even any knowledge we might have of female anatomy, physiology, psychology, or history. The image actually precedes such knowledge. It selects the aspects of knowledge we choose to pay attention to and arranges them into a pattern, because the image carries with it a whole train of associations and expectations that are preconscious and closely tied to feelings.

At the university where I teach I find two very different images of woman in the young men I meet. They continually evaluate the womanliness of women they meet according to criteria latent in these mental images. For some a woman is a coy, dependent, not overly bright individual with a particular "look," usually a look corresponding to fashion and to anatomical calculations. Such a woman does not readily disagree with a man, is apt to smile a lot in his presence, and laughs at his jokes. Other men have a different image of woman. For them, a woman is a self-directed adult, compassionate, reflective, possibly witty, but in general able to meet other adults of either sex on an equal footing. She is not better than men but she is not less either. She does not hold that men and women are the same, but she does hold that they are equal. What we have here is more than simple personality preferences. We have mental images that select and arrange for us what we see and determine the significance of our experience.

To understand this process more fully, we must recognize that underlying these images are what Gibson Winter calls "comprehensive metaphors," which function almost the way the eye does.[29] If the lens image is taken for granted because we are too busy seeing through it, the lends of the eye is taken for granted in a much more fundamental way. Any particular lens image is able to be adopted only because it rests on the deeper foundation of a comprehensive way of looking at reality: the comprehensive metaphor. Like my two hypothetical students, persons with fundamentally different lens images are operating out of fundamentally different comprehensive metaphors. Comprehensive metaphors impose a fundamental pattern on all our experience. The comprehensive metaphor I wish to examine briefly is the domination-subordination metaphor, because it characterizes our society and is at odds with the message of Jesus.[30]

This metaphor or mindset tends to break personal and social reality down into two groups: superior and inferior, with the inferior requiring direction and control by the superior. The domination-subordination metaphor leads to a variety of dichotomies, including the winner-loser dichotomy. In winning we prove our superiority and our right to dominate the defeated group. This dichotomy splits the superior from the inferior and, by extension, the stronger from the weaker. It may be difficult, for example, to convince a young man who unconsciously uses this metaphor that because women's physical strength is of a different sort than men's, it does not necessarily follow that women are poorer athletes. In the universe interpreted through the domination-subordination metaphor, stronger means superior and dominant.

These dichotomies—superior-inferior, winner-loser, stronger-weaker —find their way into our everyday language, as when in popular speech certain individuals are named "losers" and others "winners." Winners are those who are able to dominate. They are the ones on top of things. In domination-subordination thinking, we have the spatial imagery of those on top and those on the bottom, higher to lower, superior to inferior. Also is popular speech we have a range of expressions about being ahead or getting the advantage, as in a race. Of course, we speak of the arms race where we must be ahead of the Soviets. Thus images from the playing field are used in the political arena.[31] *Clout* is another popular word that fits into domination-subordination thinking, combining the imagery of a baseball bat and a prehistoric club.

The imagery that emerges from this comprehensive metaphor seems to be at odds with the gospel. Think for a moment of the word *one*. In sports, the one usually means number one, the victors, those who have dominated their inferiors. We have all often seen winners shouting ecstatically, "We're number one!" In the Eucharistic liturgy, however, the word *one* is used repeatedly to signify the human unity of those joined together by the Spirit of Jesus. Here *one* means communion and unity.

Once we see the metaphor, once we become aware of it as a lens, a fundamental shift takes place in our consciousness: we begin to see and think differently. For young people, this is the point when they can begin to select images more appropriate to them. Instead of competitive and dominating images, they can consider the usefulness of cooperative, collaborative images, life-giving images, images of mutuality. If not explicitly images of public action, such images all emphasize solidarity and common ideals, and ultimately, a public voice.

We Christians can help youth appropriate consciously the imagery of our tradition, the imagery of mutuality, of the call, (for the Hebrews a call to be a sign in the world, as it was for the early Christians), of the journey of freedom, the walk through the desert, of exile. What of our primal imagery of the sharing of bread and drinking from a common cup as a sign of unity? To these let us add the imagery of resistance to injustice, oppression, falsehood, and selfishness. This imagery is also present in our scriptures, though in a more subtle way. We may find them most explicitly set forth in the Book of the Apocalypse.

Assistance Toward Action

Much has been written about action for young people. Among the writers are teachers in high schools who are convinced that secondary school, both public and private, should include some exposure to social needs in ways that enable students to help alleviate those needs. Without in any way negating their value, we can discern in such projects a utilitarian tinge and a potential danger of becoming, for the young engaged in them, another in a series of requirements for graduation. Other writers about action are rethinking pastoral strategies for the sacrament of Confirmation. They believe that no one should receive Confirmation who has not shown a willingness to translate the gospel message of compassion into deeds. Though I am certain that some young people discover in these Confirmation projects human needs far greater than their own and so come to enlarge their capacity for empathy, such projects are also in danger of becoming another in a string of requirements with which young people have to cope.

Many religious groups now offer youth various forms of action, some of them intended to alleviate social problems. Among such activities are walks, runs, or bike races for various causes, raising money through sponsors who donate a certain amount of money for each mile walked, run, or biked. These activities raise consciousness among those who actually engage in them and also among those who sponsor them. Again, without denying the value of such forms of action, I wish to point out their limitations. These external actions do not necessarily lead to understanding the core or the complexity of the problem. In the end, they only deal with the problem from the perspective mainly of fund-raising, which is the perspective of money. It is telling that such forms of action seem to be preferred by young people living in a consumer culture.

The problem with such strategies of action is they do not generally deepen the participants' understanding of an issue. Participants expend considerable energy but do not question or probe the structures that give rise to the problem. For example, a few years ago a group of young people from the town of Cairns on the northeast coast of Australia set out riding power mowers down the coast a thousand miles to Sydney, in order to raise money for cancer research. Were the energies of these young people trivialized in the planning and execution of this action? Did the event help them become aware that they live in a country whose uranium mining makes it a key link in the chain of causes of cancer in our time? Could young people walk to raise money, say for Covenant House, and still not question whether their lifestyle might be in subtle collusion with the same social systems that created the need for Covenant House? I have in mind such behaviors as patronizing pornography or creating alienation among peers by mistreating friends or acquaintances.

The sort of action I believe most important for young people today is the action that uncovers injustice. Martin Luther King, Jr., showed us that certain actions cause no trouble because they leave the structures of injustice untouched or unexposed. Such structures tend to be invisible or to appear innocuous. Quiet weapons factories dot our landscape, but when people climb the fences surrounding them to expose the horrors being prepared in these same "peaceful" locations, they cause trouble indeed. When King protested racism in the U.S., he was accused of being a troublemaker, though he was actually exposing injustice.

Another aspect of the action I propose for youth today is action that is public. While young people can meet many quasi-private needs, by taking meals to shut-ins and visiting the lonely, for example, these needs are the task of whole communities and not just of young people. But relevant public action for young people is action in which they make their own concern for the common good visible and articulate. The following example illustrates action that is public in this sense: Every Wednesday, a small group holds a vigil outside the laboratories of the Sperry Corporation on Long Island, where guidance systems for nuclear missiles are developed. Some Wednesdays there might be just one or two persons there, handing out leaflets and holding a sign asking the workers to question what they are doing. Such activity comes from the personal commitment of a small group trying to touch the spirits of those working at Sperry. But their action also takes place in public. It does not get much publicity but still it remains public. It is also symbolic action in that it questions the morality of the entire corporation. These witnesses at Sperry might get more satisfaction doing good works instead of their lonely vigil, but they have seen the value of action in the public sphere and have chosen to commit themselves to it as part of a public plea for sanity.[32]

If action is to be a way of helping young people achieve a public voice, we will have to develop forms of true participation for youth and distinguish them from forms of illusory participation. An example of illusory participation is military service, where the price of participation is unquestioning obedience. True participative forms provide access to decision-making, so that all participants have a voice in the way the organization or action is run. True participative forms generally question their own taken-for-granted procedures and respond to the questioning. Not all who work with young people are comfortable with such participation on the part of youth. However, participation is the way people grow, and if we work with young people, we must grow together with them.

Clearly, the questions raised here are complex. I share them in hope that many others will continue to reflect on them. Originally my chief concern was the place of youth in the church. But to understand their situation fully, one must examine their position throughout society. This consideration opens up many searching questions. One of the most important questions relates to the forms of action appropriate to young people. In a sense this entire book addresses that question. Though I have examined the question of action briefly here, I explore in the following chapter what I call "youth politicization," as a way of further examining the potential of young people for action in the public sphere and of tapping their spiritual energies for the benefit of the common good. We all need to be enriched by these energies.

---

[1]Tillie Olsen, *Silences* (New York: Delacorte, 1978), p. xi.

[2]Ibid., p. 23.

[3]Ibid., p. 16.

[4]Ibid., p. 31.

[5]Elizabeth Schussler Fiorenza, *In Memory of Her* (New York: Crossroads, 1983), p. xvii.

[6]Paulo Friere, *Cultural Action for Freedom* (Cambridge: Harvard Educational Review, Monograph Series 1, 1970), pp. 3-4. Note also the irony of a nineteenth century British strategy towards a "domesticating literacy":
Some of those [in the 19th century] arguing that the poor must be able to read the Bible, as a means to their moral improvement, overlooked the fact that there is no way of teaching a man to read the Bible which does not also enable him to read the radical press. The consequent disillusion was considerable. Again, others argued that the poor should be taught to read, in the interests of moral improvement and working efficiency, but that there was no need at all to teach them to write, beyond the capacity to append a signature, since it was evident that they would have nothing to communicate on their own account (Raymond Williams, "Communications Technologies and Social Institutions," in *Contact: Human Communication and Its History,* ed. Raymond Williams [London: Thames and Hudson, 1981], p. 230).

[7]Gustavo Gutierrez, *We Drink from Our Own Wells* (New York: Orbis, 1983), p. 11.

[8]Olsen, p. 27.

[9]Rod Stewart, "Young Turks," (London: Riva Music, 1981). See the analysis of this song in Michael Warren, *Communications and Cultural Analysis* (Westport: Bergin and Garvey, 1992), pp. 74-78.

[10]Richard Rodriguez, *Hunger of Memory* (New York: Bantam Books, 1982), p. 138.

[11]William Beardslee and John Mack, "The Impact on Children and Adolescents of Nuclear Developments," in *Psychosocial Aspects of Nuclear Developments* ed. Rogers and Weinberg (Washington, D.C.: American Psychiatric Assn., 1982), pp. 64-93.

[12]See Robert Jay Lifton, "Beyond Nuclear Numbing," *Teachers College Record* 84, no. 1 (1982): 15-29.

[13]Olsen, pp. 41-43.

[14]See Craig Wolff, "Playing for Keeps," *The New York Times Magazine,* 30 October 1983, pp. 32ff. This is a lengthy descriptive essay about high school football's evolution in our time. See also, Christian Bromberger, "Le football [soccer] met a nu les antagonismes majeurs de nos societes," and Patrick Mignon, "Racismes et violences dan les tribunes," both in, *Le Monde Diplomatique* (Juin 1992), pp. 10-11.

[15]See "Death and Violence," Chapter 5 of Fred M. Hechinger, *Fateful Choices: Healthy Youth for the 21st Century (* New York: Carnegie Corporation 1992), pp. 140-171.

[16]See Edward Wynne, "Adolescent Alienation and Youth Policy," *Teachers College Record* 78, no. 1 (1976): 23-40. Wynne's piece may help one get started paying attention to demographic information about youth. I caution readers on some of his conclusions. See also U.S. Bureau of the Census, Current Population Reports, P-23, No. 114: *Characteristics of American Children and Youth: 1980* (Washington, D.C.: U.S. Government Printing Office, 1982).

[17]Thomas Merton, *Gandhi on Non-Violence* (New York: New Directions, 1965), pp. 7-8.

[18]Andrea Dworkin, *Our Blood* (New York: Perigee Books, 1981), p. 32.

[19]See George Steiner, *Language and Silence* (New York: Atheneum, 1967), pp. vi-x.

[20]Ibid., pp. 34-35.

[21]Ibid., p. 97.

[22]Ibid., pp. 99-100. Thomas Gallagher documents a similar debasing of the Irish by the British ruling class during the Irish famine in *Paddy's Lament* (New York: Harcourt Brace Jovanovich, 1982).

[23]An important commentary on this process is George Orwell's "Appendix: The Principles of Newspeak," in *1984* (New York: New American Library, 1983), pp. 246-256.

[24]See Thomas Merton, "War and the Crisis of Language," in *Thomas Merton: The Nonviolent Alternative,* ed. Gordon C. Zahn (New York: Farrar, Straus, Giroux, 1980), pp. 234-47. Merton deals with military distortions of language in many of the essays in this fine collection. See also, Robert McAfee Brown, "The Debasement of Language," *The Christian Century,* 6 April 1983, pp. 313-15; Rollo May, *Power and Innocence* (New York: W.W. Norton, 1972), pp. 65-77.

[25]*The New York Times,* 6 June 1984, p. A8.

[26]Cited in Brown, p. 314.

[27]A valuable study of this question is in Gibson Winter, *Liberating Creation* (New York: Crossroads, 1981). Gibson's work provided background for the chapters on images and metaphor in Michael Warren, *Communications,* op. cit.

[28]Here I am following Charles Davis, "Religion and the Sense of the Sacred," Catholic Theological Society of America *Proceedings* 31 (1976): 87-105, esp. 87-91. Further background can be found in, Catharine MacKinnon, "Pornography, Civil Rights, and Speech," *Harvard Civil Rights—Civil Liberties Law Review* 20 (1985): 1-70.

[29]See Winter, pp. 1-28.

[30]This metaphor is explored in Matthew Lamb, "Christian Spirituality and Social Justice," *Horizons* 10, no. 1 (1983): 32-49.

[31]See George Orwell's treatment of this transformation in his brief essay, "The Sporting Spirit," *Selected Writings* (London: Heinemann, 1947), pp. 159-162.

[32]Action as a special sort of language is a key aspect of the theory of expressivity I am working from here. This aspect needs extensive further treatment. Those interested in reflecting further might want to study the theory of symbolic action found in the public symbolic action of Daniel Berrigan. A provocative essay on the search for new forms of expression in the midst of crisis is Czeslaw Milosz, *The Witness of Poetry* (Cambridge: Harvard University Press, 1983), pp. 79-97. See also, "Justice Catechesis and the Problem of Action, Chapter 8 of M. Warren, *Faith, Culture and the Worshiping Community,* pp. 154-170.

Chapter 3
Youth Politicization: Awareness Plus Action

Since the publication of *Youth and the Future of the Church* (1982), the chapter that has received the most attention is the one entitled, "Youth Ministry: Toward Politicization." Even so, it was more of an introduction to the question of what "public" means and how youth workers can pay more explicit attention to youth's place in society. The following chapter develops some of the pertinent theoretical issues. Though some may find the treatment overly theoretical, we cannot properly face the implications of politicization for action unless we are willing to examine these theoretical questions carefully.

The politicization of youth means more than simply the relationship of young people to different political parties.[1] In its broad sense, politicization has to do with the relationship of youth to the polis, that is, to the sphere of human affairs. One of the key tasks in human development is eventually to emerge from the tightly circumscribed world of the domus, from the world defined by the walls of the home, into the neighborhood, and then into the town or city, and into an ever-widening sphere that comes to one's attention bit by bit: the geographical region, the nation, the continent, the hemisphere, and finally the world as it involves the relationships among all these elements. Although such a process can and does take place physically, as when a child goes off to school the first time, or geographically, as when a family moves, it is still far from being politicization.

For a move from one horizon to another to be politicization, it must be marked by two features: awareness and engagement. Awareness involves conscious awareness of how the world "works"; without it, one lives submerged in social reality. Freire describes such a lack of awareness as a "semi-intransitive consciousness."

> Men [sic] submerged in the historical process are characterized by a state I have described as 'semi-intransitivity of consciousness'.... Men of semi-intransitive consciousness cannot apprehend problems situated outside their sphere of biological necessity. Their interests center almost totally around survival, and they lack a sense of life on a more historic plane. The concept of semi-intransitivity does not signify the closure of a

person within himself, crushed by an all-powerful time and space....
Rather, semi-intransitive consciousness means that his sphere of perception is limited, that he is impermeable to challenges situated outside the
sphere of biological necessity. In this sense only, semi-intransitivity represents a near disengagement between men and their existence. In this
state, discernment is difficult. Men confuse their perceptions of the
objects and challenges of the environment, and fall prey to magical
explanations because they cannot apprehend true causality.[2]

Freire's semi-intransitive consciousness is a mythical consciousness which accepts the world and society as a given, imposed as prior to
a person's freedom, and not open to critical scrutiny.[3] The consciousness
needed for politicization is one that is searching out the formative
processes which create reality. Since reality is socially constructed
through human effort, such a consciousness sees every aspect of it as
open to a critical examination of its fitness or validity. In such a consciousness, no aspect of reality is closed to questioning, and every
aspect is open to the possibility of reconstruction.[4] Politicization, however, moves beyond consciousness to engagement and acceptance of an
active role in the polis. One moves from observer to participant. Indeed
behind Freire's language of transitivity is a grammatical metaphor of
subject acting rather than of object being acted upon. Freire describes
the engagement process thus:

As men [sic] amplify their power to perceive and respond to suggestions
and questions arising in their context, and increase their capacity to
enter into dialogue, not only with other men but with their world, they
become "transitive".... Transitivity of consciousness makes man "perme-
able." It leads him to replace his disengagement from existence with
almost total engagement.[5]

As Freire describes it here, the engagement process seems to
involve only a way of knowing without any necessary master plan for
social structures, that is, without ideology.[6] However in actual life, "load-
ing" critical awareness-toward-action with a specific set of aims is a second but inevitable step.[7] In other words, as an explanation of how social
reality works, politicization is an epistemology; as a kind of engagement,
it moves toward ideologically committed forms of action. For example,
the oligarchs of Guatemala and El Salvador know just as their opponents
do, how their own socio-economic world works, but their understanding
is filtered through a very different ideology, one committed to maintain-
ing their own positions of privilege. The engagement side of politicization
is motivated by more than epistemology. It is fueled by attitudes and values that represent a stance.

The Gradual Move Toward Critical Consciousness

It seems clear that not all adults become politicized in Freire's sense of entering into self-directed dialogue with, and engagement in, their world. For that matter some never become politicized even briefly, in dealing with a single issue.[8] What percentage of adults are in fact capable of being politicized remains an open question. One could raise the same question about youth. Ultimately, the question must be raised, since politicization in my sense here is action freely taken toward emancipation. It can be proposed but never imposed. Politicization, in any biography, is a possibility, not a certainty.

The question of timing is also important. When should those charged with the education of young people move more consciously toward politicization, toward the questioning of socially induced values and understandings? At what precise age does one become capable of critical thinking? Probably, the move to critical consciousness must be done gradually and be progressively encouraged, so that as youth move into their late teens, they become aware of the social construction of reality. Whatever the specific problems of timing, a mind unable to think critically, is inappropriate in a young person approaching the age of twenty, and particularly so in those pursuing a college education. What follows examines first some ways in which the consciousness of youth is kept de-politicized and un-critical and secondly, some ways in which they are conditioned more for passivity than for engagement.

Domesticating Youth's Consciousness

Formal education is in part a process of examining how the world works and is for most persons, in the West at least, a sort of rudimentary politicization, if only in the sense that one has moved into social structures beyond the home. What actually happens is that one moves into a broader system of socialization. An emerging body of educational theory is now scrutinizing schooling sharply.[9] As sociologists of education, these scholars use critical analysis to discern how educational institutions succeed in retailing to young people a mythicized view of reality. As Michael Young describes their work, these social analysts begin

> with the assumption that those in positions of power will attempt to define what is to be taken as knowledge, how accessible to different groups any knowledge is, and what are the accepted relationships between different knowledge areas and between those who have access to them and make them available. It is thus the exploration of how these processes happen, since they tend in other than pre-literate societies to take place in and through educational institutions, that should form the focus of a sociology of education.[10]

Although Young notes that this exploration of the social workings of educational institutions is as yet in its rudimentary stages, the ironic situation it exposes is evident: educational institutions themselves can foster a mythic consciousness.

In our time, the politicization of young people is a dilemma compounded by other forces, particularly electronic media, influencing decisively the consciousness of persons of all ages in Western society, as Kennedy Fraser has pointed out in her essay, "The Fashionable Mind."[11] Such forces contribute widely to the actual decline of adulthood.[12] As pervasive as these electronic shapers of consciousness may be, my judgment is that the young are especially susceptible to them because the young have less perspective. Theirs is an emerging consciousness. More than one mythic world must be broken before a person develops the skepticism needed for critical consciousness.

Predictably, a keen awareness of the susceptibility of youth to advertising can be found in the literature generated by the marketing industry about "the teen market." Utilizing the studies of Piaget and Kohlberg among others, as well as their own sophisticated statistical measures, marketing researchers are assuring their clientele that gaining the attention of young people and influencing their needs has long-lasting effects on product preference and thus on profits.[13] The effects of such orchestrated programs to influence youth are not without their political implications as Paulo Freire has pointed out.

> Perhaps the greatest tragedy of modern man [sic] is his domination by the force of these myths and his manipulation by organized advertising, ideological or otherwise. Gradually, without even realizing the loss, he relinquishes his capacity for choice: he is expelled from the orbit of decisions. Ordinary men do not perceive the tasks of the time; the latter are interpreted by an "elite" and presented in the form of recipes, of prescriptions; they drown in leveling anonymity, without hope and without faith, domesticated and adjusted.[14]

Freire's concerns are similar to those of Marie Wynn[15] and Neil Postman,[16] two recent critics who have analyzed the specific dangers of television to the consciousness of children and adolescents. In *The Plug-in-Drug*, Wynn reviews extensive research on the effects of television on young children in order to warn parents about the kind of passivity fostered by this medium.

> [A]n awareness of television's potentially pathogenic influence on young children's ways of thinking and behaving may lead parents to reconsider their acceptance of television as an inevitable part of their children's lives. It may change their focus from what their children are watching to why and how much they are watching, and what they are missing as a

result. An understanding of the changes in child rearing brought about
by the availability of television as a sedative for active and troublesome
preschoolers, changes that lead to poorer socialization of children, may
cause parents to decide that their difficulties as parents are ultimately
increased, not alleviated, as a result of their use of television as a source
of relief. And finally, a consideration of the inroads television makes into
family life, its effects on meals, conversations, games, rituals, may per-
suade parents that the price of accepting television as a force in the family is too high to pay.[17]

Postman hypothesizes that in an age of television young people are
moving back toward an oral culture where, in order to present a narrative, one had to immerse the self in the spoken word, with a consequent
loss of objectivity.[18] The written word, on the other hand, depends on
some degree of critical detachment and on the ability to think about
thought. The age of television reverses the revolution-toward-reflection in
human consciousness set in motion by Plato's banishment of the poets
and their oral culture from the Republic, in order to make way for a new
order of abstraction and analysis by means of the written word.

Far from scorning oral culture or even television, Postman proposes a self-adjusting theory of education that will maintain a proper tension
between oral and written cultures.[19] In a time dominated by electronic
curriculum, schools, according to Postman, must compensate by stressing literacy and articulateness. Moreover, the loss of the analytic power
and articulateness demanded by literacy has political import, as
Postman suggests in the following passage.

[W]hen we put the non-linguistic bias of the media together with their
bias toward one-way communication, the result is something more than
maladjustment symptoms. We may have a near-lethal problem in social
pathology. For example, there is no doubt that the new information environment provides access to knowledge about events and people all over
the world. Through electronic media everyone's affairs become our business.... But if we live in a global village, it is a strange village indeed:
though we live in it, we are both mute and powerless. In fact, we do not
live in it. We observe it, and can exert no influence upon it. Even worse,
we cannot even decide what portions of the village or aspects of its life
we will see, or the points of view from which we will see it. These decisions are made by the frame of a television screen, by the values of a
television director, according to the biases of a television network.[20]

While there is no guarantee that literacy will lead a person to the
sort of awareness and engagement that characterize politicization, there
is a guarantee that without literacy, without an active ability to come to

grips with the world of ideas through both understanding and articulation—there can be no politicization.

Problems of Engagement

The question of the politicization of youth in our time is compounded when one examines the way young people are inserted into the major institutions that affect their lives. In the face of these institutions youth tend to be both powerless and voiceless, in short, to be thoroughly domesticated. Domestication as the opposite of politicization is best understood through the image of the domesticated animal, the creature that has made the transition from being "wild," i.e., dependent for its survival on its own resources and direction, to being "tame" and capable of residence within the domus, where its survival is assured through the beneficence of its human masters. The domesticated animal does not forage; it has moved to a state of passivity, where it is simply fed. In return for this assurance of regular sustenance, the one attribute the domesticated animal must exhibit is predictability. The unpredictable animal is considered not housebroken, not fully broken to the will of its masters and essentially not worthy of life within the domus. In my judgment, the image of domestication is an apt one for delineating the role of youth in many of the social structures affecting them.

Here I will focus most attention on youth's place in two institutions, the school and the church. However, I wish to begin with a more compelling example of youth's powerlessness and voicelessness in our society: conscription and military service. Even though military service in the United States is not currently on a conscription or draft basis, as a program held in readiness, it illustrates vividly some of society's overall program for young people. Although most countries allow for conscientious objection and alternative forms of service, conscription starts from a premise of the duties of young people rather than of their rights. Before the voting age was lowered to eighteen, conscription in the United States was imposed on those who were disenfranchised because of their age. Even today, registration for the draft, the preliminary to conscription, is imposed on the date of one's eighteenth birthday, before most young people have cast a vote. This situation demonstrates elements of age discrimination, that is, of the projection onto a certain age group of presuppositions and expectations not in the best interests of that group. Since so few church-related people and so few educators have questioned this practice, it appears that many adults presume voicelessness and powerlessness as a normal condition of the young. This question will be treated in more detail in Chapter 9, which deals with militarism and peacemaking.

Returning to the effects of schooling on the politicization of youth: Over the past twenty years numerous critics have examined the consequences for youth of the policies and procedures that characterize schools. Philip Jackson's *Life in Classrooms*,[21] in particular, seems to have called the attention of many to the covert messages of high school routines. Soon after the publication of Jackson's book, Frederick Wiseman's film, *High School*,[22] illustrated vividly Jackson's "hidden curriculum," which serves to foster passivity and inarticulateness among teens.

In his study of adolescence in the U.S., from the time of the early republic,[23] historian Joseph F. Kett sheds light on the way the high school gradually came to control more and more of the lives of youth, especially through extracurricular activities. By 1910, the University of Chicago High School, for example, had assigned faculty advisors for every student club and had regulated meeting times. "Music clubs met on Monday, the science and library clubs on Tuesday, and so on. The tentacles of control extended to dances too, for to discourage students from patronizing sleazy dance halls in the neighborhood, the school conducted its own socials."[24] Kett notes that

> public high school officials spoke of like-spiritedness, but they often imposed like-mindedness. The years between 1900 and 1920 witnessed the virtual destruction of student autonomy wherever the high school was transformed into a total environment for teenagers. Student self-government conveyed the semblance of power without its substance, for principals kept an absolute veto over anything worth vetoing. For those middle-class young people privileged to attend high school, the status of studentship was becoming nearly coterminous with that of youth. Of course, it was still possible for a young person to acquire a political education without playing out the charade of student self-government, (but it would have to be acquired on the streets).[25]

Several studies of high schools over the past quarter century pinpoint the same problem in our time that Kett finds in the schools of the 1920s. In 1974, the Panel on Youth of the President's Science Advisory Committee reported its conclusions in *Youth: Transition to Adulthood*.[26] This report notes how since the 1920s two of the three interest groups in the typical high school, administrators and faculty, have organized in increasingly sophisticated ways to serve their self-interest.[27] Administrators have promoted bureaucratization in order to establish a hierarchy of responsibility and routine procedures for control. Administrators of high schools and school districts came to preside over larger and larger bureaucratic superstructures. Simultaneously faculty members moved to protect their own autonomy by setting up professional associations and unions. Thus, since 1945, adolescents in the United States have been enveloped by large, complex organizations with converging (but sometimes conflicting) aims toward bureaucratic and professional control. As administration and faculty became better organized, students have tended to become mute, at least in any organized way, about their position in the system.

In 1976, the National Panel on High School and Adolescent Education reported the same problem: "The schools baby-sit, at very high cost during the day, the nation's nighttime baby-sitters."[28] Although this report deals with immensely complex social problems clearly beyond the scope of any single social institution, its underlying concern that youth be given more responsibility for their own lives is an important concern for politicization. A glimpse of the direction in which the National Panel Report points can be found in the following passage.

> Schools have had in the past, and continue to have, a custodial style largely because they are seen as custodial institutions by much of the general public. Adolescents are children who are to be kept off the streets and out of the labor market. Within the school the student is given limited options about how to spend his or her time, with little freedom for the kind of social peer experience that young people strongly desire. A single pattern of behavior is rewarded, that of academic excellence, the hallmark of which is more often obedience than independent thought. Perhaps most enervating is the system of rules and procedures which dominate in school life, and which the adolescent has seldom had an opportunity to participate in developing.
>
> The treatment of adolescents as dependents needing direction and guidance from supervising adults, in fact, tends to retard their maturity. Yet precipitate removal of all constraints can lead to personal bewilderment and a sense of incompetence bordering on the traumatic. What seems clear is that present secondary schools have unnecessarily prolonged modes of operation which have not kept pace with the maturation of the adolescent population. Keeping youth in infant bondage destroys their capacity to assume responsibility for the consequences of their acts at an age appropriate to their physiological and psychological development.[29]

The panel's specific recommendations are worth the attention of all concerned with youth's place in the high schools.[30]

The prospectus originally developed by Dr. Theodore Sizer for his study of high schools offered some useful clues to youth's potential place in the structure of the secondary school.[31] Eventually published as *Horace's Compromise*, Sizer's study examined youth's place in high

school from an important perspective: their freedom. Former Dean of
the Harvard Graduate School of Education and former Headmaster of
Phillips Andover Academy, Sizer proposed to study the "teacher-student-
subject triangle" and the outcome of constructive confrontations
between teacher, student, and subject in various learning settings.[32] He
hypothesized that students must have a place in working out with teachers some agreement about their mutual enterprise. "Agreement means
active engagement in a triangle which becomes a safe harbor for dispu-
tation and disagreement, for the making of mistakes, and for the cau-
tious (often painful) exploration of how a student, a teacher, and a subject begin to confront one another."[33] Sizer identified the freedom of
choice for young people as an important, if overlooked, feature of effective secondary schooling.

Churches also tend to foster passivity and reward predictability in
young people. In the second half of the nineteenth century, Christian
churches progressively rewarded subservience and developed a bias
against intellectual and spiritual precocity.[34] Church leaders set out trivial, even mindless goals for young people. Among the vapid, ludicrous
church activities recommended to youth in the late nineteenth century
were responsibilities such as "running errands for the pastor."[35]

In her 1976 report of interviews with a thousand teen women,
Gisela Konopka found that eighty-three percent of those belonging to
youth organizations had dropped out, because these groups were seen
as too domineering and not offering them enough of a true leadership
role.[36] In a similar vein, Merton Strommen's earlier study of the relationships among various generations of Lutherans[37] found that over half of
Lutheran young people aged 15-23 reported they had no influence on
the decisions being made by their congregations, which excluded them
from positions of leadership and influence.[38] Such positions tended to be
in the hands of those over thirty years of age. So little place did these
young people find for themselves in an adult church that up to one-half
agreed with the statement that "hardly anyone in the congregation would
miss me if I stopped going."[39] Church-related efforts with youth today still
offer too little opportunity for growth in self-direction and leadership. Operating as they do out of the same cultural biases about youth as do
schools and other social agencies, church organizations for young people often make the same errors.

Conclusion

I believe that politicization is an appropriate ideal for those growing
toward adulthood and for those seeking to guide them, but that the
major institutions dealing with youth tend to direct them away from polit-

icization. I also believe that religious conviction devoid of political interest is possible but inappropriate. These beliefs lead me to look for agencies capable of fostering the intersection of religious and political awareness and engagement based on religious conviction. Do such agencies exist? What, for instance, are the potential roles in politicization of the school, religious education, and the church? Schools may seem the best suited for fostering the critical consciousness necessary for politicization. However, schools tend to be used to retail to young people the consciousness of those controlling school policy.[40] Also, the compulsory nature of schooling in our society tends to limit it as a zone of freedom so necessary for politicization. Further, as agencies for training intelligence, schools cannot appropriately foster political engagement.[41] I doubt one can become critically conscious solely through study. Engagement is at least as formative of such a consciousness as is study.

What of religious education? Can it foster politicization? To what degree of engagement is religious education prepared to commit itself? How many religious educators, for example, would embrace Donald Williams's view that "the most immediate challenge facing *religious education* [italics mine] is to so educate that increasing number of churches, families, individuals and church-related institutions and groups become active and effective participants with God in the struggle to humanize life in the arena of public affairs."[42] I believe Williams claims too much for religious education. He proposes that

> the overarching aim of religious educators should be to foster political resocialization in all of the agencies engaged in the task of political socialization to the end that persons socialized therein might learn to acquire and exercise the requisite political power to most fully humanize their lives and the lives of their fellowmen, in the light of such Judeo-Christian values as love and justice.[43]

In asking *religious educators* to assume such decisive influence in shaping policy for the agencies engaged in the task of political socialization, Williams seems to inflate the goals of religious education. My own judgment is that youth politicization is most possible when it uses modest strategies to deal with specific issues: Gathering young people voluntarily during their own time, to search out information on issues; establishing a climate of trust within which points of view can be confronted, clarified, judged, and revised; following through on programs of action based on informed decisions and an awareness of risks. Such a modest program would lead young people step by step toward activity that informs.

Clearly, religious education has as part of its task education in the crucial juncture between the religious and the socio-political spheres of life. However, like schools, it too seems appropriately limited to the sphere of education. Actually, if politicization is a multi-faceted and life-long task, no single agency can complete the process. What is needed is collaboration among many agencies to develop critical awareness-toward-engagement.

When first reflecting on youth politicization in a religious setting, I theorized that the most appropriate framework for it was not religious or Christian education but youth ministry. Youth ministry is the work of a community of believers concerned not solely for the education of its young but for their fuller human development, of which education is but one component.[44] The four components of youth ministry are: the ministry of the word, that is, the meanings that bind the community together as they confront their current situation in the world; the ministry of worship, that is, the community's celebration of its common understandings and of the bonds they create; the ministry of guidance and counsel, including education; and the ministry of healing, by which the community offers healing both to its own members and to a world seriously out of step with its own vision of human existence.

However, not all youth ministries follow this outline. Careful thinkers will also see that a key variable in my theory involves the kinds of meanings that bind the community together in the first place. As these understandings differ, the thrust of communities differs widely, as is the case of the political understandings (in the narrow sense) of the fundamentalist evangelical churches, some of which have banded together as the Moral Majority.[45] My initial selection of youth ministry as an appropriate context came partly from a conviction that since youth politicization involves both a critical consciousness and active engagement, it goes beyond education and must be more than education. Actually the ideal context for such politicization would be an intergenerational community modeling active commitment to justice out of religious faith.[46]

For those working with youth within various agencies in our society, the matters proposed here as part of a new agenda will demand close attention in the form of further reflection, study, and reformulation. Above all, they call for redirecting our efforts with youth toward freedom. For too long adults working with youth have had the tendency "to view the nature of adolescence as endogenously programmed and the typical behavior of individual adolescents as determined by intrapsychic forces."[47] Refocused attention toward the social forces affecting young people, including a focusing of the attention of young people themselves on the way these forces work, will be a major step toward allowing youth opportunities for significant action toward emancipation, action which could become a lifelong commitment.

---

[1]A lucid treatment of this point and of several other aspects of youth politicization is in Paul Surlis, "Towards the Politicization of Youth: Some Reflections," *The Living Light* 18, no. 4 (1981): 253-260. Dr. Surlis' suggestions have been of particular help to me in developing my own approach to this topic.

[2]Paulo Freire, *Education for Critical Consciousness* (New York: Seabury, 1973), p. 17.

[3]Charles Davis, "Toward a Critical Theology," in William McClendon, *Proceedings of the 1975 Meeting of the American Academy of Religion* (Missoula, Mont.: Scholars Press, pp. 213-19.

[4]Ibid., pp. 213-14.

[5]Freire, p. 17.

[6]I am clearly using *ideology* in a neutral sense to express "life stance." In his essay cited above, Charles Davis, by defining ideology in a pejorative way, makes critical reflection opposed to all ideology.

Critical reflection is, in a second way, emancipatory in being a critique of ideologies. Ideology is a distortion resulting from social structures of domination and violence, analogous to the structures of repression in the individual as uncovered by Freudian psychoanalysis. The critique of ideologies on the social and political level carries out the functions performed by psychoanalysis on the individual level. In other words, just as on the individual level, a critical consciousness demands that we enquire how far stances, responses, assertions and decisions are distorted by the blind spots and inhibitions resulting from repression, so also on the social level criticism requires us to uncover the hidden, systematic distortions produced by repressive social structures. A process of simple interpretation is not enough when dealing with the products of social consciousness. Critical reflection must also develop genetic explanations to account for the ideologies that trammel social communication. (Davis, p. 214)

For a different view of ideology and one closer to my own angle of vision, see Juan Segundo, *The Liberation of Theology* (New York: Orbis, 1976), p. 154.

[7]My position is similar to that of Trent Schroyer. He states:

[T]o have a theory broad enough for a societal critique is not to have an `instrument to guide praxis.' A historical theory must be interpreted in regard to specific historical conditions and hence between theory and praxis there is a crucial mediator of judgment. It is illusory to believe that any critical theory can simply be a `tool' in the hands of any class. Between theory and praxis there is a crucial phase of political program formulation which requires not only theoretical clarity but practical judgment about specific life worlds (Trent Schroyer, "Marx and Habermas," *Continuum* I, no. 1 (1970): 52-64, esp. p. 60, n. 15.

[8]There is a sense in which one cannot be nonpolitical, since to overlook totally the political is itself a political act of putting the world into the hands of others.

[9]Persons wishing to get a grounding in this literature might well begin with the following "earlier" essays: articles by Michael Apple, Dwayne Huebner, Maxine

Greene and William Pinar in *Curriculum Theorizing: The Reconceptualists*, ed. William Pinar (Berkeley: McCutchan, 1975); Roger Dale et al., *Schooling and Capitalism: A Sociological Reader* (London: Routledge and Kegan Paul, 1976); J.B. MacDonald and E. Zaret, eds., *Schools in Search of Meaning*, (Washington, D.C.: Assn. for Supervision and Curriculum Development, 1975); Michael F.D. Young, ed., *Knowledge and Control: New Directions in the Sociology of Education* (London: Collier-Macmillan, 1971); Michael Apple, *Ideology and Curriculum* (Boston and London: Routledge and Kegan Paul, 1979).

[10]Young, *Knowledge and Control*, p. 32.

[11]Kennedy Fraser, *The Fashionable Mind: Reflections on Fashion* (Boston: David Godine, 1985), pp. 145-159.

[12]George W.S. Trow, "Reflections: The Decline of Adulthood," *New Yorker* 17 November 1980, pp. 63-171.

[13]As examples of what may be found in this overlooked literature, here are some examples culled from a four-year period: George P. Moschis and Roy L. Moore, "Decision-Making Among the Young: A Socialization Perspective," *Journal of Consumer Research* 6 (September 1979): 101-112; Roy L. Moore and Lowndes F. Stephens, "Some Communication and Demographic Determinants of Adolescent Consumer Learning," *Journal of Consumer Research* 2 (September 1975): 80-92; Scott Ward, "Consumer Socialization," *Journal of Consumer Research* 1 (September 1974): 1-17; Gerald J. Gorn and Marvin E. Goldberg, "The Impact of Television Advertising on Children from Low Income Families," *Journal of Consumer Research* 4 (September 1977): 86-88; George W. Schiele, "Reaching Teens with Same Message," *Advertising Age*, 26 February 1979, pp. 24-26, 29; George Moschis, "Teenagers' Response to Retailing Stimuli," *Journal of Retailing* 54, no. 4 (Winter, 1978): 80-93; Ronald W. Stampfl, George Moschis, and Joseph T. Sawton, "Consumer Education and the Pre-School Child," *Journal of Consumer Affairs* 12, no. 1 (Summer, 1978): 12-29.

[14]Freire, pp. 6-7.

[15]Marie Wynn, *The Plug-in Drug* (New York: Bantam, 1977).

[16]Neil Postman, *Teaching as a Conserving Activity* (New York: Delta, 1980). See also his, *Amusing Ourselves to Death: Public Discourse in the Age of Show Business* (New York: Penguin Books, 1986).

[17]Wynn, pp. 246-47.

[18]Postman, *Education* pp. 29-46.

[19]Ibid., pp. 15-25.

[20]Ibid., p. 80.

[21]Philip W. Jackson, *Life in Classrooms* (New York: Holt, Rinehart, and Winston, 1968).

[22]Frederick Wiseman, *High School* (Boston: Zipporah Films, 1969). See reviews in Life, 12 September 1969; *Phi Delta Kappan*, September 1969; *New Republic* 21 June 1969; *New Yorker* 18 October 1969; *Saturday Review*, 19 April 1969.

[23]Joseph F. Kett, *Rites of Passage: Adolescence in America, 1970 to the Present* (New York: Basic Books, 1977).

[24]Ibid., p. 184.

[25]Ibid., p. 187.

[26]James S. Coleman, ed., *Youth: Transition to Adulthood* (Chicago: University of Chicago Press, 1974).

[27]Ibid., pp. 76-81.

[28]National Panel on High Schools and Adolescent Education, John H. Martin, Chairman, *The Education of Adolescents* (Washington, D.C.: U.S. Government Printing Office, 1976), p. 5.

[29]Ibid., pp. 22-23.

[30]The major recommendations are found in Chapter Two.

[31]Theodore Sizer et al., "A Study of High Schools: A Proposal," mimeographed, March 1981. See also Theodore R. Sizer, *Horace's Compromise: The Dilemma of the American High School* (Boston: Houghton Mifflin, 1984), pp. 154-71 and 205-13.

[32]Sizer, "A Study," pp. 9-14.

[33]Ibid., p. 11.

[34]Kett, pp. 173-211. See in particular his summary, pp. 210-11.

[35]Ibid., p. 194.

[36]Gisela Konopka, *Young Girls: A Portrait of Adolescence* (Englewood Cliffs, N.J.: Prentice-Hall, 1976), pp. 129-36. See also the interview with Dr. Konopka in *Youth Ministry: A Book of Readings,* ed. M. Warren (New York: Paulist, 1977), pp. 196-203.

[37]Merton Strommen et al., *A Study of Generations* (Minneapolis: Augsburg, 1972).

[38]Ibid., p. 255.

[39]Ibid.

[40]An important example of how effectively consciousness shapes curriculum is documented in Frances FitzGerald's examination of history textbooks in the United States. Her study, originally appearing as a *New Yorker* series, shows how thoroughly filtered is the view of United States history found in many texts, some of which retained the same editorial distortions during seventy years of revisions. See Frances FitzGerald, "Onwards and Upwards with the Arts: History Textbooks," *New Yorker,* 26 February 1979, 5 March 1979, and 12 March 1979. For an extension of FitzGerald's work, see David R. Olson, "On the Language and Authority of Textbooks," *Journal of Communication,* Winter 1980, pp. 186-96.

[41]In a fine essay, Fred Newmann argues for the place of a serious political

engagement in secondary schools, pointing out the many non-academic action programs provided in schools: music, sports, clubs, student government, etc.—but not political enablement. See Fred M. Newmann, "Discussion: Political Socialization in the Schools," *Harvard Educational Review* 38, no. 3 (1968): 536-545, esp. 539.

[42]Donald F. Williams, "Religious Education and Political Socialization," *Religious Education* 65, no. 5 (1970): 388-89. Although I disagree with some of Williams' positions, his article stands as one of the few pieces dealing with this topic in an in-depth way. See also James Hitchcock, "Fathers and Sons: the Politics of Youth." *Review of Politics* 34 (1972): 158-73.

[43]Ibid., pp. 389-90.

[44]See, M. Warren, "Youth Ministry in Transition," *Youth and the Future of the Church*. (Minneapolis: Winston-Seabury, 1982), pp. 8-16.

[45]See Frances FitzGerald, "A Reporter at Large: The Reverend Jerry Falwell," *New Yorker*, 18 May 1981, pp. 53-141. Note especially Falwell's attempts to limit the consciousness of his congregation and the limited access to information found at his Lynchburg Bible College in pp. 96-112 and 120-24. See also, Frances FitzGerald, "Reflections: Jim and Tammy," *The New Yorker* 23 April 1990: 45-87.

[46]The sort of intergenerational community I have in mind can be found spelled out in C. Ellis Nelson, *Where Faith Begins* (Atlanta: John Knox, 1967). The entire book spells out Nelson's understanding of how an entire community can be critically conscious. See especially Chapter V, "Faith and Perception," which deals with the community's ability to interpret its current situation in the world.

[47]John P. Hill, cited in Joan Lipsitz, *Growing up Forgotten: A Review of Research and Programs Concerning Early Adolescence* (Lexington, Mass: D.C. Heath, 1977), p. 7.

Chapter 4
Facing the Problem of Popular Culture

This chapter is written out a desire to empower readers to think more deeply about the various influences in the lives of our youth—and indeed, in our own lives. I do not intend any diatribe against electronically communicated messages—what here I arbitrarily refer to as popular culture. My purpose is to expose a problem easily overlooked by us all, simply because as part of our everyday life, the problem tends to get overlooked as just another feature of the landscape we see every day. For most readers, the key step will be take another look at the problem side of culture and then work to face it more squarely. Those wishing to pursue this important issue further will find a much more detailed approach to it in my 1992 book, *Communications and Cultural Analysis: A Religious View,* published by Bergin and Garvey.

Influencing young people toward the liberation which the gospel invites us to accept is becoming increasingly difficult in the face of other powerful influences which incessantly and often effectively propose to them values quite in opposition to Jesus' way. In a society dominated by electronically communicated images, young people are continually having their lives imagined for them by means of television and film scenarios, depicting for them in vivid terms the sort of life most ardently to be pursued, often enough a life counter to that proposed or imagined for us by Jesus. The problem, however, goes deeper, since not only young people but all those who interact with them—parents, teachers, youth ministers, church leaders—are being influenced by the same "image" culture. If older people intervening in the lives of youth are themselves naive about the effects of the media, they will hardly be able to help young people resist those effects. What I offer here is an introductory reflection on the problem of contemporary culture, the sort of reflection I hope will eventually raise even deeper questions.

I begin this reflection with questions I have been asking myself, which may shed light on the problem we all face in trying to influence young people toward a committed Christian, healthy human life. The questions are: In your own effort to listen to the preaching of the gospel at the celebration of Eucharist, do those who preach it seem to be under the spell of a radical commitment to the values and way of Jesus, or are they more under the spell of our current culture, accepting without question its various assumptions? Do they accept its assumptions about the roles of the sexes, that is, the culture's sexual stereotypes? Do they accept, also without question, language games that use "national security" to legitimate any horror or that define peace as something that happens when one party is sufficiently beaten down by the other? Do they accept the culture's retailing of respectability and interpersonal warmth as the goals most devoutly to be pursued above all others?

The question of where preachers stand I have found myself asking more and more, as I have sat and listened to religious leaders supposedly strive to break the bread of the word and to call whole congregations to come alive with the hope of following Jesus' foolishness. Where do these men stand? I have asked myself. Most of what I have heard presented has seemed so directed toward individual personal comfort, so filled with reassurance, so certain that all would turn out for the best, that I have often wondered if we could be living in the same century, not to mention the same city. This has been the sort of preaching Richard Sennett might have had in mind in the following critique.

> The reigning belief today is that closeness between persons is a moral good. The reigning aspiration today is to develop individual personality through experiences of closeness and warmth with others. The reigning myth today is that the evils of society can all be understood as the evils of impersonality, alienation, and coldness. The sum of these three is an ideology of intimacy: social relationships of all kinds are real, believable and authentic the closer they approach the inner psychological concerns of each person. This ideology transmutes political categories into psychological categories. This ideology of intimacy defines the humanitarian spirit of a society without gods; warmth is our god.[1]

Slowly I began to wonder if I was expecting too much of these men. It occurred to me one day that possibly the preacher has the same basic mindset as that of the other men of his own age in this neighborhood. If the neighborhood butcher or movie theater manager or hospital administrator all met in a bar, they might all have the same basic perceptions of the world, except that one of them uses those perceptions as the undergirding onto which to superimpose a religious message. Obviously such a line of thinking is a troubling one, but one with special relevance for those concerned with the way young people think and perceive: youth ministers and educators.

Increasingly, the core question I find myself trying to face as both a professional educator and one committed to ministry is a question about how culture and education interact. If popular culture is in our time an enormous picture window showing people ever more fantastic views of what life is all about, then maybe education becomes a kind of tiny peephole not accessible to very many and at which one has to strain to see anything. How can the peephole compete with the magic picture window? The magic window is so automatic and easy; the peephole requires more effort.

And what about the mindset of the young people with which teachers and youth ministers are dealing? To what degree do we find their minds and hearts shaped by the understandings, principles, and commitments explored in the classroom or in youth programs? Are they influenced by that curriculum, or is that only a shadow curriculum compared to the real curriculum in their lives? I believe the actual, influential curriculum is formed by groups working apart from the school, usually seeking some financial advantage through catching the attention of young people. Of the many forms such curricula take, I wish here to note four as particular challenges for teachers and youth ministers:

1. The incessant and effective messages of the advertising industry, which teach young people how to view their bodies and their appearance, while shaping their preferences on a wide range of matters;
2. Some of the messages of the music industry, which when carefully attended to shock us with their brutality and crassness;
3. The political messages found, not in in-depth news reports or in editorial analysis, but in headlines alone and in the simplistic, right-and-wrong analyses in TV news shows;
4. The messages about violence that occur in a world where only might makes right.

Each of these topics represents a curriculum, not simply in contradiction to the one we espouse in our youth programs and religious schools, but in most instances effectively overriding it. Each topic deserves extensive and subtle treatment. By reflecting briefly here on each area, I hope to show how deeply this problem of offering gospel values in the face of popular culture runs in order to stimulate further reflection on the educational challenges before us.

The Curriculum of the Marketeers

Members of the advertising industry have been doing hard statistical research for years and are now making extensive use of social science research, especially that of Piaget and Kohlberg, to give a broader theoretical base to sophisticated measures to determine influences. They have also studied socialization theory, in order to determine the impact of early socialization on later patterns of consumer behavior. These people are not pernicious; they are following their profession as marketing researchers. Thus the following ad for advertising copy in *Seventeen* is based on extensive research.[2]

It's a woman's prerogative not to change her mind.

Are women indecisive? Yes and no.

Yes, they're about as indecisive as humans of the other gender.

And no, they're not as indecisive as several generations' worth of women's jokes would have you believe. Quite the contrary. In fact, a recent major Yankelovich study showed that:

• two out of every five women aged 20-34 are still using the same brand of mascara they selected as teenagers.

• More than one in three use the same brand of nail polish.

• And more than one in four use the same bath soap. In fact, in category after category, despite fads and changing trends, one thing remained unchanged:

To a surprising degree, a girl's first choice is the one she stays with.

And, more often than not, the place where she first does her choosing is *Seventeen* Magazine. Where each month, more than 6,400,000 teenage girls begin lasting relationships.

If you'd like more information, call our Advertising Director, Robert Bunge, at 212-759-8100. You'll learn why advertisers start lasting relationships in *Seventeen* too. *Seventeen*: It's habit forming.

This ad shows the care with which the advertising industry charts its long-range influence on the behavior of young people. Such influence in itself may not be pernicious; however, it does seem to be almost inevitable and certainly has a bearing on our work as educators.

Kennedy Fraser in a perceptive critical essay on fashion, has suggested what that bearing might be.

> Fashion usually is neither named nor noted but is simply the lens through which our society perceives itself and the mold to which it increasingly shapes itself. This hidden, powerful, mental sort of fashion

is thus worth taking stock of. In spite of its great parade of intellect, its support in influential places, and its mellifluous accompaniment of self-promoting public relations, the new variety of fashion pretty much shares the creed and the limitations of the frivolous, pirouetting old variety of fashion, that of dress. *The shared creed is materialistic and holds that appearances are of greater significance than substance.* [emphasis added] Among the shared limitations are fickleness, a preoccupation with descrying the will of the majority in order to manipulate it or pander to it, and a concern with the accumulation or protection of power and profit. Although all fashion looks mobile and rebellious at times, its roots are surprisingly constant: to think or act for reasons of fashion in any given field is to support that field's established centers of power.[3]

She goes on to claim that the new form of fashion tends to lead all of us to be less reflective and less able to question or critique. However, Fraser herself offers a critique that may be of special significance to an educator or youth minister.

Fashion as it exists now, whether in literature or in kitchen equipment, in neckties or in ideas, is intimately connected with money and power. This basis is by no means always apparent, and our careless, inherited assumption that fashion is spontaneous, amusing, innocent, and amateurish is likely to keep us from examining or questioning the ways in which it has evolved. The part that commerce plays in fashion is something we are often led to overlook, for the fashionable mind is well-practiced in masking a general allegiance to commerce and the status quo behind what seems to an outsider to be an appealingly individualistic enthusiasm for some particular novelty. Fashion is a skillful master of enthusiasm, and of a Pavlovian discernment of certain correspondences—between a current best seller and a potential successor, for instance—but is an inadequate touchstone in the search for honest, disinterested distinctions. These are born of an isolated, dogged, unfashionable side of the mind—a sort of gawky mental provincialism.[4]

Fraser here is describing the "programmed consciousness," which I claim to be a key educational problem and issue. Educators and youth ministers wishing to counter the programmed consciousness may need to add a loving crankiness to their gawky mental provincialism. Indeed, they will need a sharp analytic eye for this and the other three dominant curriculum areas.[5]

The Curriculum of Teen Music

For many working with youth, either in schools or in local church-es, teen music is not easy to pay attention to. Often enough, those who have heard the rhythms over and over again while spending casual time with the young have tended not to listen to the words, which may seem indiscernible to even the most attentive. When attended to, however, the messages of some songs are crass and unspeakable and worth the painful attention of those who care about the young.[6]

Obviously not all songs for the young are crass; some are quite beautiful, and anyone ready to point out those in the first category had better be ready also to point out those in the second. All this music needs to be attended to, because almost all of it is about relationships, from varied, even contradictory, points of view. I do not refer here to any particular songs because they come to seem old very quickly, and young people tend to dismiss discussions of old songs, but show quick interest in the current ones. Also, copyright managers sometimes refuse permission to cite a particular song if they know the context will be criti-cal; or they will inflate the copyright fee to a forbidding sum. However, for those interested, finding out which songs are current is easy enough, since the young are more than willing to share the current songs with adults who ask about them. I have found it helpful to ask them about songs they find particularly beautiful or particularly crass. They supply endless examples of each category and thus provide older persons the very first step in dealing with this curriculum: paying attention to its con-tent.

The Curriculum of Political Messages

A stunning example of this problem occurred in an undergraduate class I was teaching a few years ago. It was the day after we all became aware that our country had invaded Grenada, a tiny Caribbean country about a hundred miles off the coast of Venezuela. I had been dealing with the issue of conflict and conflict resolution in marriage. In that context, I mentioned the difficulty of proposing respectful styles of conflict resolu-tion in interpersonal relationships, when on a global level we keep seeing reliance, not on civilized communication, but on the resolution of conflict through armed might. At that point the war seemed to jump from the Caribbean to that classroom.

Almost all students, at least all the vocal ones, defended the action of the United States armed forces, without any questions. Now, taking sides is not something to be deplored. What I found alarming was the manner in which the sides were taken. From students at a large universi-ty, I heard the most simplistic rendition of what had happened, all cast in we-and-they terms, with the United States as the good guys and "they," the former Soviet Union, as the bad guys. We had invaded this country, they claimed, to protect the safety of our own citizens, to guard against a takeover of the nation by Cuba and the Soviet Union, and to protect our national security in an area that was "in our back yard." However, that very morning *The New York Times* had published news reports and analyses, if not contradicting, then at least questioning, each of these claims.

The question of international law did not arise at all, and when I brought it up, was dismissed as irrelevant. Fully absent from the students' position was any concern for history, for questions of national policy, or for bringing into the discussion related matters such as the troubles in El Salvador, Guatemala, Nicaragua, and Honduras. In short, they were unable to think, to work from principles, facts, and history. They seemed to be mouthing code words and cliches, to be operating out of a kind of "fashion." Kennedy Fraser also wrote:

> The excessive use of fashion as a framework for perception will ultimately warp that perception and, with it, any reasonable picture of the world. The greatest drawback of an overfashionable perception is that fashion is concerned, virtually by definition, with surfaces, images, and appearances.[7]

During that class discussion a young Shiite Moslem woman from Iran was present. She was quiet in class, unwilling to comment on life in Iran under the dictatorship of the Shah, a regime supported by the U.S. government, except to say that some of her friends and relatives had been murdered by his regime. After class, however, she came to me with the following reflection:

> Growing up in Iran we had always to read books about political and economic backgrounds of the areas we studied. We had a political sense; we were taught it, even under the Shah. Here in the U.S., all the young people I know and meet seem entirely ignorant of such questions. They are interested only to be reading of love and romance and sex. Even my friends here are this way. On the bus I see what people my age read; it is all love and romance. These students in this class do not know anything about the matters of which they talk.

She might have added that one cannot get the sort of factual information needed for an informed judgment from television news. In one city, a study of the late night news showed that in one thirty-minute segment there were fourteen commercials and thirteen stories.[8] A total of fifteen minutes was devoted to the news. The remaining time was divided between commercials (seven minutes), sports (three minutes and thirty-five seconds) weather (two minutes and ten seconds), and introductions, teasers, transitions, lottery numbers, and sign off. Foreign coverage was limited to two stories. In the face of such a curriculum those who wish to propose gospel values based on sound information have their work cut out for them.

Curriculum of Violence

In North America young people live in a subculture of violence they themselves have not named and which has not been so named by most adults they interact with. Adults tend to be aware of the problems of youth and drugs, alcohol abuse, automobile death, and suicide, but not as aspects of a single problem—violence. The violent images in the everyday language of young people suggest how deeply violence haunts their imaginations.

Those wishing to pay closer attention to this language will get some helpful leads from the following analysis of Scott Hope, which relates this language to the wider societal and global problem of violence.

[T]he post-Hiroshima generations have been the first generations which have had to live with the possibility that humankind with its inventiveness has the potential to destroy itself. Nuclear destruction, the depletion of resources, global war, ecological disasters are the common currency of our daily consciousness. We cannot read a newspaper or a magazine, view a television news program, listen to a radio broadcast, without being reminded that the world is too much with us. The individual often feels helpless in the face of that apocalyptic agenda, and in the face of that helplessness feels that she/he can do nothing to change things for the better, that she/he can but attempt to repress the implications of the daily digest of disasters. Unfortunately, out of mind is not necessarily out of sight or out of body, and the fear of the future, the fear for survival, bubbles around in the bloodstream like additional dark cells.... That fear of the future, of space, of technology goes underground, but it surfaces in some of the feelings described a moment ago, and it surfaces in many rather odd ways in our daily lives. Let me give but one example.... Have you ever noticed how... [young people] talk about feeling better [or about having a good time]? [They] talk about being bombed, smashed, wasted, wired, wiped out, blown away. Have you listened closely to the diction of our days and nights: outta sight, tripping out, blowing it, etc.... the words are taken from the lexicons of space, technology, destruction and death. I think this is not accidental, and I think this is not a consciously determined language. The fear of the future, the fear of what we have wrought in the future, the fear of what we have wrought in the post-industrial world, finds its secret ways to our tongues even when our minds choose not to deal with it.[9]

This analysis is as unpleasant as it is important. These images of destruction may be operating as a subliminal filter at a far more basic level than the gospel message about peace, overriding the messages of our schools and youth programs. Those who love the young need to notice whether the young let our programs remain neatly boxed and shelved like a set of dull novels that no one takes up willingly. Many of our young people seem to live educationally schizoid lives, such that a trash film like *Porky's* actually influences their aesthetic judgments more deeply than the works of Flannery O'Connor, Benjamin Britten, or Marc Chagall, or the memory of Jesus.

Extending the Questions

Suppose all teachers and youth ministers put to themselves the same questions I posed about those who preach: Are they formed by our culture or are they working out of a Christian vision? Is their profession something in a briefcase, to be put aside after school and then taken up again and again in five-hour segments? Are they demonstrating a probing mind, a quest for deeper understanding? Do they exhibit the questioning attitude that should mark a person in our society seeking to combine the life of the intellect and the spirit? Or are their minds and imaginations far more effectively dominated by, for example, Saturday afternoon football than by even the most basic intellectual questions? Are there any characteristics of mind and spirit that distinguish us from those inhabiting the same neighborhoods in which we work and live? If we met at the local bar would we have the same cast of intellect and spirit as persons who are laborers or administrators or public servants?

Some readers may now suspect I am heading toward some sort of despicable elitism or snobbery. That is not my intent, and I want to say clearly that I hope we can all recognize qualities of the human spirit that sometimes bring us to awe, as when the simple goodness of some young person, who might also be almost illiterate, becomes for us an example of the possibilities of human achievement. The question I am trying to raise is this: As persons working with youth, are there any commitments that come from our profession that distinguish us, just as our very professional activities are different from those of laborers, managers, or administrators?

The reason I wish to raise these questions here is that in our society, the wider curriculum being beamed at us incessantly is so pervasive, even massive, that if we do not set ourselves to resist it, we will be swept away by it. We are all liable to become creatures of the cliche, ineluctably humming in our imaginations jingles of the hucksters and storing in our memories the half-truths of the political marketeers. Could it be that a characteristic of educators in such a time must be a kind of resistance? Education for critical scrutiny and the sort of resistance it fosters will be the appropriate kind of education in Catholic schools and youth ministry programs in the future, since it is the only kind that can deal with the key cultural forces shaping the minds of our young people. I agree with Neil Postman's recent assessment of the problems affecting education in our time.

It is obvious that the major educational enterprise now being undertaken in the U.S. is not happening in the classroom but in the home, in front of the television set—not under the jurisdiction of school administrators and teachers but of network TV executives.... Television has, by its power to control the time, attention, and cognitive habits of our youth, inevitably gained the power to control their minds and character as well. This is why I call television a curriculum. As I understand the word, a curriculum is a specially constructed information system whose purpose is to influence, teach, train, or cultivate the mind and character of the young. Well, television does exactly that, and it does it relentlessly; in so doing, it competes successfully with the school curriculum. In fact, it damn near obliterates it.

Here are some facts for skeptics to ponder. The only activity an American child engages in that occupies more time than televiewing is sleeping. Using the 1982 Nielsen Report, you can estimate that, between ages 6 and 18, an American child averages about 16,000 hours in front of a TV set; that same child will spend only about 13,000 hours in school. By my reckoning, in the first 20 years of his or her life, an American child will see approximately 700,000 TV commercials, at a rate of close to 700 per week.... Children have already clocked nearly 5,000 hours of televiewing before they ever show up at school.[10]

Postman identifies five key characteristics of the television curriculum. He claims that each characteristic fosters attitudes and predispositions "antagonistic to what the school wishes to teach." According to Postman, these characteristics define the battleground on which the struggle between two modalities of education is taking place.

   1. The television curriculum is rooted in the analogic, nondiscursive visual image, given in rapid series. The average length of a shot on a network television show is 3.5 seconds, so that every few seconds a person is getting a new point of view, which again shifts to another and so on. In commercials the length of a shot is 2.5 seconds. A child watching television must process as many as 1,200 different shots an hour, or 30,000 a week for an average eight-year-old. The dominance of

such dynamic visual images tends to erode a young person's language skills and analytic skills, which demand a different level of concentration, more slow-moving, logical, continuous, and abstract.

2. The television curriculum is non-propositional and therefore irrefutable. We can like or dislike pictures and stories, but it is difficult to dispute them. Stories are not true or false the way propositions are.

Such words as true and false come out of a different universe of symbolism altogether. They are applicable to the world of exposition, in which we confront statement and counterstatement, hypotheses, reasons, refutations, contradictions, explanations, verifications, above all, where we confront ideas expressed in the form of subjects and predicates.... School... is a world dominated by subjects and predicates.... Television is a world dominated by stories.[11]

3. The television curriculum is easy. It requires no skills and develops no skills. That is why there is no such thing as courses in remedial televiewing.

Television is the most egalitarian curriculum ever devised. Everything in it is for everybody, simultaneously. And thus there can be no standard of excellence, or of competence, or even of improvement. I need hardly dwell on the consequences of such an education. Suffice it to say that such an education mocks the ideas of deferred gratification, self-discipline, and intellectual achievement, without which education is mere entertainment.[12]

4. The television curriculum is entertaining. It is an attention-centered curriculum. Its prime purpose is to keep the attention of its viewer-students. In school, when a student fails to pay attention, she/he may be removed. In the television curriculum, when the student (viewer) repeatedly fails to pay attention, the "teacher" is removed; that is, the show is canceled.
Unfortunately, the achievements of literacy, of probing reflection, and of analysis are not won through fun. They require a kind of discipline in the pursuit of skill that is antithetical to fun. Of course, the exercise of any skill is often exhilarating, even ecstatic: but even there, the word "fun" does not seem to apply.

5. The television curriculum is fragmented and discontinuous. Nothing one sees has any necessary connection with anything else. A glance at the syllabus of the weekly TV Guide shows how it is made up of discrete and at times contradictory

events. The clearest example is the television news broken up
by commercials that have no connection with news stories.
Each separate program, or commercial even, stands alone.

> Make no mistakes about it: the TV curriculum embodies a
> clear and powerful philosophy concerning the nature of reality.
> Its axioms include that history is bunk, that hierarchies are
> arbitrary, that problems have no antecedents, that the future is
> not worth dwelling upon, that randomness is uncontrollable. I
> believe the word is Dadaism. In psychiatric circles, it is known
> as chronic depression.[13]

My own conclusion from this rather scary rendition of the power of
the electronic curriculum and the relatively weaker place of the school
curriculum or parish youth program is that, for the future, schools and
out-of-school youth ministry will have to be more and more committed to
resistance as a style of education, resistance to a kind of nondiscursive,
nonanalytic cast of mind that tends to evaluate reality in terms of "I liked
it" or "I didn't like it." This will be resistance to the erosion of standards
of excellence and standards of craft, as well as to sloppy mental habits.
Such resistance will involve a commitment to intellectual discipline and
competent achievement. Resistance to what is fragmented and random
will be in the name of a commitment to finding patterns, to understanding systems, to examining contexts.

Another conclusion is that educators and youth workers will have to
develop critical perspectives on what they themselves see and hear, so
as to be able to share these with the young. Diatribes against the imagined evil monster, "media," are not only useless; they border on the
mindless. Denunciations are better replaced with skills of judgment,
skills of analysis, skills in naming how images, visual narratives, visual
cliches, and so forth actually work. As I have pointed out in other contexts, many people bring to the selection of their electronic equipment
sophisticated technical norms by which they make judgments and selec-
tions, and then they employ no norms in judging the images and messages that come to them via this equipment. I believe the task of judgment is an important part of the task of humanization in our time. Our
very work with youth ought to provide a context in which judgments
about what enhances or diminishes the humanly good become a part of
ordinary life. Does not Jesus provide us with norms by which to make
judgments about life? If he does, why are these not part of our daily living? If there are many grey areas when we encounter particular situations, why are we not at least grappling with the dilemma? As a minimal,
though not easily realized, goal for youth ministry, I propose the follow-

ing: that it have more sophistication in making judgments about what is humanly good than it has in selecting electronic equipment. I will return to youth and culture from an even broader angle in the final chapter of this book.

---

[1]Richard Sennett, *The Fall of Public Man* (New York: Vintage, 1978), p. 259.

[2]*The New York Times,* 23 April 1980, p. D24. Repeats of such ads are easily found in current issues of *Advertising Age.*

[3]Kennedy Fraser, *The Fashionable Mind: Reflections on Fashion,* (Boston: Godine, 1985), pp. 145-146.

[4]Ibid., pp. 149.

[5]See, Hechinger, *Fateful Choices,* "Image and Competition vs. Nutrition and Exercise," pp. 173-187.

[6]See my own brief essay, "Speaking to the Songs," in *Youth and the Future of the Church,* pp. 68-73.

[7]Fraser, p. 148.

[8]Jack Thomas, "Channel 7's Not-so-new News," Boston *Globe* 8 October 1982, p. 35.

[9]Scott Hope, "The Unchurched Young Adult," unpublished paper, pp. 10-11.

[10]Neil Postman, "Engaging Students in the Great Conversion," *Phi Delta Kappan,* January 1983, p. 311.

[11]Ibid., p. 313.

[12]Ibid.

[13]Ibid., p. 314.

Chapter 5
Zone of Liberation: School

Although in the following pages I treat a particular zone of ministry with youth, the secondary school, I encourage readers whose ministry with youth is largely outside of schools and not centered in school-type instruction not to jump past this chapter. The ideas which follow can be applied to multiple zones of youth work—and even to ministry to and with adults.

One dare not speak glibly of the special contribution high schools can make, especially since some critics claim the high school has become a totalistic institution controlling too many aspects of a young person's life.[1] One report, as we have seen, claims that "the schools baby-sit, at very high cost during the day, the nation's nighttime baby-sitters."[2] This particular report recommended that compulsory daily attendance in high school be reduced to an academic day of 2-4 hours and that the school's basic role be that of fostering intellectual abilities,[3] It recommended the school do fewer things but do them better.

However, in 1972 Catholics received from the American bishops a pastoral on Catholic education that eventually served to inflate the claims of Catholic schools.[4] Schools were to be characterized by community, message, and service. As a result, some principals sought to screen out teachers who were not Catholics, while others screened out those who were not Christians. In some instances—far too many in my view—the school thought itself to be a surrogate church. Such inflated goals represented a serious mistake, because they forgot that the school could never be church: at best it could be an agent in the mission of the church and a sign of the church, but only then if it became a zone of truth. To be a house of truth, a school must at least be somewhat of a pluralistic institution where good persons from varying perspectives attempt to encourage themselves and others toward wisdom.

Indeed, one of this chapter's theses is that the role of the church-affiliated high school is to be a voice in the wilderness, that is, to offer quality education in the context of counter-cultural values based on the gospel. One of the problems all schools—public, private, and parochial—face is that they represent a socialization thrust of society, by which the rising generation is induced into the mores and values of the culture. It is too easy for schools to become the cheering squads leading the cheers for the contemporary culture. The best schools raise serious questions about this culture, critique it, and put it in perspective—they offer some critical distance from which to view culture. Church schooling should do this in a special manner, since it is based on Jesus' extensive set of principles that turn popular wisdom on its head.

A proper understanding of the high school recognizes it is a societal entity at the same time that it may be a church entity. Perhaps it actually functions much more as a societal institution under state control and as a business operation, involved in fiscal questions of cash flow, salary increases, and increased sources of funding, than as a sign of the community of those following Jesus' way. If true, this position must be faced squarely and realistically, not buried under a mountain of rhetoric based on the seriously flawed document "To Teach as Jesus Did."[5]

In the following pages, I seek to examine three major directions in which some schools are struggling to move in their effort to be a humanizing voice in the wilderness.[6] I will introduce each of these directions in the form of a question, because ultimately those guiding particular schools must struggle to answer these questions.

Can the high school in our day foster a critical consciousness that moves young people away from the special naivete so dangerous in our time? We all know the meaning of naivete, a word that has long been synonymous with youth. The word connotes being innocent of and ignorant about the complexities of key areas of life, especially of interpersonal life. A classic area of naivete is sexuality, and the word is often used to refer to sexual ignorance. Another classic area of naivete is ignorance of the possibilities of evil in interpersonal relationships. We find naivete at this level explored in such works as *Billy Budd, Lord Jim, Othello, Rigoletto,* and for that matter in *Romeo and Juliet.* This is the naivete we have been dealing with traditionally and with some success. In some of our urban settings, even children become "street wise" quite early. However, there is another level to ignorance and innocence that in our time is more dangerous than the old naivete, because it has more disastrous effects.

This is the naivete that is ignorant, not about the complexities of interpersonal life but about the world of wider human affairs. This new naivete is a lack of awareness about the power of institutions, about the social structure that shapes one's life, and about the cultural norms one tends to accept unquestioningly. This second-level naivete is stubborn because we tend to overlook it. However, one cannot meet the challenge of being a Christian in our times without stepping out of this second-level naivete. One cannot understand the meaning of evil in our time by understanding it only at the personal and interpersonal levels. The great horrors of our century have all been horrors perpetrated at the systems level, at the level not of the individual gone mad but of the social or-

ganism gone out of control. We can be aghast at insanity at the individual level but stare unblinkingly at the face of insanity at the level of public policy. There can be no critical consciousness without an examination
of reality at this wider social level.

Critical consciousness is thoughtfulness and reflectiveness, not just
at the personal level, but at the social system level also. Hannah Arendt,
the Jewish philosopher, has pointed out to us in her analysis of Adolf
Eichmann the true scope of personal evil when it is linked with evil social
systems.[7] In what she subtitled "A Report on the Banality of Evil," she
emphasized that Eichmann was neither a monster nor a demon. He was
simply thoughtless, unreflective about the consequences of his deeds.
He followed cliches, popular wisdom about being loyal to one's superiors,
about getting along by going along, about the superiority of patriotism to
all other considerations. He questioned nothing of the system he was in.
As he himself said in his own defense, "Where would we have been if
everyone had thought things out in those days?" Hannah Arendt came to
a conclusion that critical thought was one of the activities that can help
people abstain from the sort of evil Eichmann represented. By critical
thought she meant more than the pursuit of knowledge. Knowledge in
itself does not make one thoughtful. Arendt proposed a kind of thought
that calls into question all structures, all codes of conduct, producing an
interior dialogue that produces a conscience. As she put it, "when everybody is swept away unthinkingly by what everybody does and believes
in, those who think are drawn out of hiding because their refusal to join
is conspicuous and thereby becomes a kind of action."

A high school has to stand beside Hannah Arendt's position
because of schooling's capacity to call into question so much of the
taken-for-granted, business-as-usual procedures of our society. Christian
social teaching of the last twenty-five years alone puts those of us who
accept it into a critical stance about many of the policies of our own government, particularly policies toward the poor and about our weapons
production. Some of our schools do not disseminate these teachings,
because some of our administrators and teachers are not aware of them.
A critical consciousness is aware of the formative processes that create
every society and thus.every individual. It pokes into the conditions that
create particular norms and policies the way a child would poke a snake
to see if it is still alive. Such creative skepticism tends to dissolve the
apparent necessity of the given world so it can be more human.

The opposite of this critical awareness is a mythicized consciousness that accepts the social order as a given, open neither to question
nor to creative reconstruction.[8] If church schools are to be faithful to their
religious tradition, they have no choice but to foster critical consciousness because gospel-based social teachings demand it in big doses.

Further, if these schools are to be faithful to their students and call them to adult fidelity, they must help them gradually become aware of the great systems in which they are submerged and about which they tend to be unaware. Many people in society profit from the submerged consciousness of youth, just as they profit from our unwitting collusion in not challenging the submerged consciousness of our young people.[9]

Fostering critical consciousness will probably demand changes in both curriculum and teaching style. It would be ironic if a group of educators not affiliated with church schools, Educators for Social Responsibility, led the way in developing critical teaching methodologies, while those in religious schools, whose sacred texts demand such methodologies, lagged far behind. Social commentator, Frances FitzGerald has documented how high school history texts present U.S. history as a survey only of dominant opinions and dominant personalities, especially those of presidents, ignoring the way dissent and the proper checks and balances among conflicting interests helped shape the nation.[10] In her view, this history curriculum has masked the important place of conflicting points of view in our past.[11] All schools, particularly church-affiliated ones, should be keenly interested in such examinations of curriculum. Beyond curriculum, the process of critical teaching seems to call for a critical dialogue among teachers and students, posing questions that have no simple answers. Courses with a one-sided stress on "the facts" stifle critical consciousness. A matter more delicate than that of curriculum and teaching style, but also potentially more important, is that of school policy and the sort of room it allows for dissent. The problem is illustrated in the following press report.

> A State Supreme Court justice has determined in a ruling that the principal of Holy Family High School of South Huntington, L.I., [Long Island] acted in an "arbitrary and capricious" manner when he suspended the school's 17-year-old student president from classes for breaking his rule against speaking to striking lay teachers. The principal, the Rev. James P. Kelly, had accused the student leader, Susan McCabe, of insubordination, which according to the school's handbook of rules and regulations is an offense comparable in seriousness with immorality and theft. Miss McCabe spoke to two of the school's ninety members of the Lay Faculty Association... during an eight week strike.[12]

As untypical as this example might be, it serves to raise the issue of how school rules and regulations can serve to quash disagreement. If religious fidelity demands a capacity for dissent,[13] then religious schools have to provide channels for dissent as part of their education in a religious heritage.

Can the high school in today's audio-visual society lead young people to radical literacy? All of us face enormous difficulties when dealing with this question, which opens up some specific ways of moving our schools toward critical consciousness. I would like to describe some of these difficulties and then deal with some overlooked implications of the issue of literacy. Most educators do not need evidence of declining literacy; it is a national problem. Some high school graduates cannot express themselves in a coherent sentence. Others can but choose not to bother. Students in my memory have never been great spellers. However, some recent students not only cannot spell correctly but they also cannot be bothered trying. They rarely say so, but their body language says "so what"? The problem goes even further. What does it mean when a person's handwriting screams out: I defy you to read this? What does it mean when the person you ask to read his/her own handwriting cannot decipher it? It means at least in part that written communication is not seen as worth the effort. It means that more and more of our degree holders are leaving our institutions lacking a fundamental ability crucial for the functioning of educated people in a civilized world: the ability to reflect on the written word and to express oneself in writing. I judge this problem to be of immense symbolic significance and to be connected with the basic nature of the school.

In his book, *Teaching as a Conserving Activity*,[14] Neil Postman sees young people today moving back toward an oral culture, where people are immersed in the spoken word, either repeating the narrative, or listening to it. One cannot step apart from an oral narrative the way one can from a narrative on the printed page. An oral culture is somewhat deficient in objectivity and high in subjectivity, deficient in analytic ability and high in descriptive ability. As I noted in Chapter Three, Plato realized this and that is why he banished the poets from his republic. He sensed that the world was ready for a revolution in thought by means of the written word. He wanted to foster the kind of critical detachment made possible by the written word. Plato wanted his republic to be characterized by the ability to think about thought. He banished the poets in order to make way for a new order of abstraction and analysis by means of the written word.

Postman wants schools to maintain a proper tension between oral and written cultures.[15] Today we tend to be so immersed in narratives, especially through electronic media, that as a culture we tend towards a diminished analytic ability. Try, for example, to summarize a particular plot line after viewing an hour of a commercially televised drama and then to examine it for coherence. More importantly, how often do we step back afterwards and analyze the way a particular plot portrayed men or women or violence or the poor, or professional people or single people or married people? I am suggesting here that television viewing does not

foster an ability to analyze what has been seen. Another and quite important example can be found in the music teens listen to, memorize, sing,
so often without ever becoming consciously aware of the meaning of the
words.[16] At its most ridiculous extreme, this uncritical immersion in electronic events creates a person like Chance, the gardener in Jerzy Kozin-
ski's novel *Being There*, whose statement of life's purpose is "I watch."

In a culture awash in such forms of narrative, the matter of literacy,
analytic ability, and articulateness becomes more, not less, important.
Many students I meet possess a diminished ability to think analytically or
even to put together a reasoned argument. The tendency of my own
undergraduate students is to make a statement of personal position and
then to launch immediately into a narrative of some personal experience
illustrating that position. Here I am not disparaging my students but
explaining the scope of the problem educators face in fostering critical
thinking. Neither do I disparage narrative ability,[17] but rather call attention
to the erosion of analytic capacity taking place in a time of heightened
narrative. This erosion has religious and political import.

Can one be a Christian appropriately in our times and be mute
when it comes to the ability to analyze and reason? As a follower of
Jesus can one be adequately informed about the issues by watching the
seven o'clock news on network television? When an individual does not
care to name the world and sees no value in discussing it, this is an indication that the person is so totally immersed in the socially constructed
world that it can only be assimilated, but not addressed. Is it not also
possible that those young people who cannot express thought in two
consecutive coherent sentences cannot do so partly because it seems
too little worth the effort? Lurking behind youth's lack of care about their
ability to say anything in writing, is, I suspect, an unconscious realization
that in most areas of their lives they have no significant voice. In almost
all the institutional structures that affect them, including church and
school, they tend to have no power. The world is almost totally taken out
of their hands, except the world of their peers, the power of sex, and the
power of purchasing (or shoplifting). And these latter areas are the areas
where they are exploited by the marketeers.

Literacy is important because an illiterate public is vulnerable to
manipulation by astute people who can use language in such a way as to
disguise their programs of social control. The spoken word tends to go
past us so quickly that we do not have time to reflect on how it is shaping our consciousness. However, the written word can be examined, analyzed, and critiqued because we can keep it before us and ponder. It is
not so slippery as the spoken word.

My concern here is the close connection between critical consciousness and literacy. I agree with Paulo Freire that unveiling social

reality is a first step to literacy and literacy of the most powerful kind. On the other hand, the mythicized, submerged consciousness sees little point in articulation. I am also hinting at a distinction made by Lawrence Cremin between inert literacy, which enables one to sign a document or to recognize a written document, and "liberating literacy, in which a growing technical competence is combined with expanding motivation, expanding need, and expanding opportunity."[18] Liberating literacy gives people access to written materials that "can open people's minds to change, new ideas and influences, to new goals and aspirations." Such literacy empowers people for a lifetime.

However, as Patricia Graham notes, literacy in our time must mean more than the capacity to read and write.

> Through literacy, we enlarge the range of our vicarious experience, both through our command of written materials and through formulations of new ideas demanded by the rigors of writing and speaking.... to learn, to express, to decide, to do all elements in the definition of literacy . . . together permit us to become more autonomous individuals, less circumscribed by the conditions of social class, sex, and ethnicity into which we are born.[19]

When we think about the demands a high school makes on its students—for promptness, for compliance with reasonable rules, possibly for subservience, possibly for attendance at this or that function—one can at least wish that if we are to make any demands on our students in our schools we make them first in the direction of literacy and the sort of informed judgment that arises from a liberating literacy.

Is it possible for a high school to be a center for the study of peace and a place for young people to become committed to nonviolence?

Is this a possibility in a violent society whose government threatens death and destruction in many areas of the world and whose national economy is based on the profits from the production of the tools of death? Is such a goal possible for high schools, especially church-related ones, anywhere in the North America where so many of the parents of our students make their wages in these industries, where so many of the large contributors to our schools and universities have their hands in the weapons till, through their financial investments? I believe that we can and that we must.

A school that celebrates nonviolence, that studies it, that honors those who have helped us understand it, that attempts to educate students to the presence of so many overlooked forms of violence in our society, that calls its students to nonviolence as a life stance, such a school is different. Some non-church-affiliated groups, like Educators for

Social Responsibility, have far outshone religious schools in their work to teach the young how to live non-violently.[20] A religious school wishing a more radical gospel orientation will have to adjust many of its policies, especially its attitude toward competitiveness. In an essay entitled "The Moral Function of the School," Jerome Kagan addressed this complex matter.

> In contemporary society, the relentless seeking of power, friends, fame, wealth, and love has lost its status as a sin; these goals have become rather prizes to obtain. The modern definition of unworthiness is failure to gain these resources. Put plainly, it is extremely difficult for an adult who is poor, powerless, and lonely to feel virtuous because s/he knows s/he has resisted the lusts of a corrupt society.[21]

Kagan's essay examines the kinds of expectations society has for young people, especially the way society defines success. He claims that "our reverence for the maximal actualization of individual talent, despite its praiseworthy democratic intentions, has created its own form of elitism, for we award more value to characteristics only a few can obtain than to dispositions within the competence of the vast majority."[22] As a result, Kagan notes a "chronic anxiety among many teens" in the face of the pressure to succeed, especially where success is spelled out in financial terms. He claims

> it is within the power of the school to ameliorate the bouts of anxiety and despair that permeate the mood of many American adolescents. The apprehension originates in the unwelcome realization that one's personal value is too dependent on the achievement of peers. The yoking of virtue to successful competition makes rivals of friends, creating occasional hostility among them.[23]

> I believe the schools can play an ameliorative role by providing opportunities for adolescents to persuade themselves of their virtue through acts whose benevolent consequences are not so dependent upon chance, the vicissitudes of peer and adult opinion, or the relative competence of others.[24]

As an example of the sort of behavior he has in mind, Kagan mentions acts of kindness that embody a mood of compassion. Not everyone can write great music or be scientific, but "because all are capable of honesty, it does not arouse us emotionally, and we are reluctant to award it distinction. For some, a moral life is the only sphere where the need for a personal domain of expertise can be gratified."[25] Psychiatrist Robert Coles has explained to teachers that they cannot give A for character, though if they could, some would be there fighting their way to the top of the heap for it.[26] If we cannot give A for character, we can recognize it and celebrate it. We can also celebrate and recognize the following attitudes of heart: kindness, restraint on aggression, honesty, and a reasonable blend of pride and humility.

I have offered here some very idealistic goals. I do not believe that they are out of reach, if only we would move toward these humanizing goals modestly but persistently, realistically but creatively, gradually but surely. I have been struck by the vision for schools of a Jesuit educator, who worked for some years in a high school in San Salvador, where he saw some of his fellow teachers assassinated because of their teaching about justice and where six close Jesuit friends were also murdered. Charles Beirne calls for teachers in church schools to address three focal areas:

1. Help our students to deepen their faith experience at each level of their personal development.
2. Challenge them to create an intellectual life that makes them learners for life, persons who love to read, persons who can think clearly and express themselves coherently.
3. Nudge them out of the nest of the school and into the community when the times comes for them to get involved in their communities. Help them become part of other communities, and help them reflect on this involvement so that they can integrate these experiences into their very beings.[27]

In sum, "the effective advocate for social justice in contemporary society [schools] is an endlessly patient, prudent, conscientious and even ironic person who labors persistently."[28] And what of the religious goals of the schools? Have I neglected them? No. The entire discussion has been about them. Move toward fostering critical consciousness, toward liberating literacy, and toward a commitment to nonviolence, and everywhere the word will be out that Jesus is present in their midst.

---

[1]See Michael Apple, *Ideology and Curriculum* (Boston: Routledge and Kegan Paul, 1979); John I. Goodlad, *A Place Called School* (New York: McGraw-Hill, 1984); Theodore R. Sizer, *Horace's Compromise: The Dilemma of the American High School* (Boston: Houghton Mifflin, 1984); Ernest L. Boyer, *High School: A Report on Secondary Education in America* (New York: Harper & Row, 1983).

[2]National Panel on High Schools and Adolescent Education, John H. Martin, Chairman, *The Education of Adolescents* (Washington, D.C.: U.S. Government Printing Office, 1976), 5.

[3]Ibid., pp. 13-14.

[4]National Conference of Catholic Bishops, *To Teach as Jesus Did* (Washington, D.C.: United States Catholic Conference, 1972).

[5]Some of the document's problems are surveyed in Mark Heath, "To Teach as Jesus Did: A Critique," *The Living Light* 10:2 (1973): 284-95; more recently, Michael Warren, "The Mission of the Church and Local Church Practice," *The Living Light* 28:2 (1992): 145-157.

[6]The image of the voice in the wilderness is, of course, an allusion to John the Precursor and his own prophetic message of justice and of hope for the oppressed. For a good treatment of the social context of John's call for justice, see John Howard Yoder, *The Politics of Jesus* (Grand Rapids, Eerdmans, 1972), pp. 26-30.

[7]My account of Arendt's thought here is based on James Bernauer, "Eichmann Twenty Years Later," *Commonweal*, 31 July 1981, pp. 436-38.

[8]Charles Davis, "Toward a Critical Theology," in William McClendon, *Proceedings of the 1975 Meeting of the American Academy of Religion* (Missoula, Mont.: Scholars Press), pp. 213-29.

[9]See Paul Surlis, "Towards the Politicization of Youth: Some Reflections," *The Living Light* 18, no. 4 (1981): 253-60.

[10]See Frances FitzGerald, "Onwards and Upwards with the Arts: History Textbooks," *New Yorker*, 26 February 1979, 5 March 1979, 12 March 1979.

[11]Michael Apple has examined a similar tendency in science curriculum to mask and downplay the role of conflict in scientific inquiry. See "The Hidden Curriculum and the Nature of Conflict," in *Ideology and Curriculum*, pp. 82-104.

[12]"Judge Rules Against LI Principal in Suspending Pupil during Strike," *The New York Times*, 17 November 1981, p. B6.

[13]For an overview of the biblical tradition of dissent and its impact on Western thought, see Herbert N. Schneidau, *Sacred Discontent* (Berkeley and Los Angeles: University of California Press, 1977).

[14]Neil Postman, *Teaching as a Conserving Activity* (New York: Delta, 1977).

[15]A brief but provocative essay that complements Postman's work is Walter Ong, "Literacy and Orality in our Times," *Journal of Communication*, Winter 1980, pp. 197-204. Ong offers a helpful analysis of levels of orality.

[16]See "Speaking to the Songs," in Michael Warren, *Youth and the Future of the Church* (New York: Seabury, 1982), pp. 73-78.

[17]A well-nuanced position that analytic ability can be buttressed by narrative and astute use of metaphor and other imaginative elements is, Kieran Egan, *Imagination in Teaching and Learning* (Chicago: University of Chicago Press, 1992).

[18]Lawrence A. Cremin, *American Education: The National Experience* (New York: Harper & Row, 1980), pp. 492-493.

[19]Patricia A. Graham, "Literacy: A Goal for Secondary Schools," *Daedalus* 110:3 (Summer 1981): 119-34, at p. 130.

[20]See, Linda Lantieri, "Creating Non-Violent Schools: Beginning with the Children," *Blueprint for Social Justice* 46:3 (December 1992) [Loyola Univ. Box 12 New Orleans, LA 70118-6195]. Ms. Lantieri is the Coordinator of the Resolving Conflict Creatively Program, developed by Educators for Social Responsibility.

[21]Jerome Kagan, "The Moral Function of the School," *Daedalus* 110, no. 3 (Summer 1981): 151-65, at p. 160.

[22]Ibid., p. 163.

[23]Ibid., p. 161.

[24]Ibid., p. 162.

[25]Ibid., p. 163.

[26]Robert Coles, "On the Nature of the Character," *Daedalus* 110 no. 4 (Fall 1981): 131-43.

[27]Charles Beirne, "Educating for Justice in a Complex World," *Origins* 20:45 (18 April 1991): 729/31-35, at 731.

[28]Padraic O'Hare, "Religious Education for Social Justice," *Religious Education* 75, no. 1 (1980): 86.

Chapter 6
The Teacher's Ministry of Liberation

Chapter Four discussed the problem of the two curricula, in which the formal curriculum of a school or youth program is becoming increasingly a shadow curriculum made more and more ineffective by the powerful messages being given by way of electronic sources. Chapter Five outlined some of the ways schools might counter the prevailing commercially produced culture. This chapter brings teachers into the discussion. Although the following pages refer to teachers and their specific work, almost all these reflections on the teacher's ministry of liberation also apply to a youth minister working with young people outside schools—in parishes, for example. I encourage readers to apply this chapter's ideas to their own pastoral work. Though the context addressed here may be specific, the principles are universal.

A teacher's ministry of liberation with youth needs to be grounded in a special attention to fidelity. Seeing the words, youth and fidelity, joined this way, many adults will immediately reflect on how unprepared young people seem for commitments and how casual their infidelities can be. However, my own focus here will not be so much on the kind of fidelity our youth must develop as on the matter of our own fidelity, as teachers, to young people. Do we pledge fidelity to youth? Do we profess it? In our time, what does it mean to be faithful to young people?

These are keenly important questions for anyone who is a teacher but even more so for those who are religiously motivated. When I spent a day working with a small group of church high school teachers and administrators on the dimensions of youth ministry needed in a high school, I asked the group to reflect on how they themselves perceived their profession. How, exactly, would they describe what they did? Obviously some would say, "I'm a teacher" or "I'm an assistant principal" or a counselor. But I wanted to know if there were any deeper answers. Some said "I am assistant principal for curriculum supervision" and "I coordinate the work of the various department heads, supervise all new teachers, and so forth." But I wanted something deeper yet. I asked, "Is there any other way of describing your profession?" and someone said, "Well, I guess I am in language arts, because as a science teacher I deal with language and also because teaching is a performing art." An administrator then said, "Yes, you could say that I am in management, because much of what I do is managerial: educational management." But I still kept asking, "What is the deepest level of what you do?"

I was trying to find out whether they could locate education in a place that would highlight certain features of education that can be easily overlooked. Actually, I wanted to bring out the similarity between counselors, who may not see themselves as educators, and doctors, who are not educators, and administrators and teachers, who are educators, and mothers and fathers, who also are. I wanted to suggest to them that they are all in the caring professions. Education is one of the professions of care, and to forget it is to lose touch with something fundamental in the profession. When teaching loses touch with caring, it is in danger of moving in the direction of assembly-line production, following the worst features of technocracy.

That was an introductory point in my presentation that day. However, when I got back to my university campus, my own statements haunted me. I asked myself, "Is it true?" Are my own activities fundamentally about caring—or about influencing? I have always wanted influence with young people so as to propose sane goals and humanizing, Christianizing ideals. I asked myself that day, which was more fundamental in life: influence or care? If I had to choose between the two, which one would be more basic to my own value system and self-understanding? I was not able to decide; each seemed basic but in different ways.

I had never thought about the distinction before. During that day I found myself analyzing my activities with youth from each of these angles. Finally, late in the day as I walked across the parking lot to my car, I realized that I was asking the wrong question. By forcing myself to choose between influence and care, I was creating a false choice. The two are not discrete: they are complementary. What I actually wanted was the influence that comes from care, from perceived care. Those we perceive as caring for us also have a special influence on us and vice versa.

I believe that fidelity to young people in our time begins with a quality of care, of perceivable care, in those who would seek to influence them towards good. The importance of adult influence born of care appears to be especially significant in our day when we see an epidemic of self-destructive behavior among teens. For example, suicide is the third leading cause of death in the 15-24 age group, after accidents and homicide. The rate for young adults (age 20-24) more than doubled between 1968 and 1976. In 1955 four out of every 100,000 persons aged 15-24 committed suicide; in 1975, twelve out of every 100,000 persons aged 15-24 committed suicide; by 1985 the rate had risen to almost thirteen per 100,000. This is more than triple the 1955 rate. For males, the 1988 rate was 21.9 per 100,000; for white males only, it was 23.3. And for every individual who succeeds, a possible 50 more try.[1] Those of us who work daily with teens know that this is only the tip of the iceberg, since as Tony Manero says in *Saturday Night Fever*, "There are ways of killing yourself without killing yourself." These statistics confront us with the need to re-examine the way we pay attention to young people. We can for instance be more aware of self-destructive patterns of behavior and be more attentive to signs of deep-seated depression. However, I do not wish to dwell on such specifics. For now, all I want to suggest is that fidelity to youth in our time involves a capacity for care on the part of adults intervening in their lives.

Precisely how one expresses caring must be worked out individually. Whatever we do however, our fidelity-as-care must be built into our profession as educators, instructors, administrators, or counselors. Fidelity to youth does not mean offering care without instruction. It does not mean offering comfort and encouragement devoid of any intellectual challenge or offering an escape from the kind of competence needed to be adult. But neither does it mean offering instruction without care—that is, instruction reduced to the mere performance of tasks, the imposition of routines fostering the teacher's ease rather than the student's challenge. Perceived care, then, is the mode in which our fidelity to youth is worked out. It provides the context in which teaching as a ministry with youth can function. It is needed before young people are willing to award us any significant influence in their lives. There is no formula for developing perceived care. The very perception of care comes from unwitting clues we all give as to what is really in our hearts. This quality of care can be worked on only indirectly. However, there are two important tasks in our fidelity to youth that can be worked on directly. These tasks are, first, a ministry to the gifts of youth and, secondly, a ministry to the transformation of youth.

Ministry to Gifts

Teachers who are life-givers are those who attend to the emerging creative edge of a young person's life; they notice where young people are especially alive. The question I love to ask teachers is: Tell me about the special talents of the young people you meet. One can answer that question only by pointing to particular persons. One has to name individuals and then explain how one has been paying attention to their strengths rather than to their weaknesses. This amounts to a connoisseurship of the human, an aesthetic sensitivity to human beauty and possibility. For any of us to do this, we must have the eye of an artist, which is the eye of a lover. We know that those who have an eye to our gifts and especially to our emerging or latent gifts are those who love us deeply. Possibly the adult sense of being loved comes when our unknown selves are discovered by another and then reflected back to us in affection.

In the life of each young person there are areas of competence and skill in which they take immense pride and joy. Not to know those areas is not to know the person. Not ever to ask the question about these areas is to be asleep to others. Erik Erikson writes of the striving for competence that dominates a child's life starting about age eight. I myself have been astonished at the high degree of competence young people can achieve at young ages. Which of us has not admired children's skill on skis, on skates, on the trampoline, on the parallel bars, at the guitar, the flute or piano, on the dance floor, on the stage? Have we ever been in awe at their achievements in poetry; in their knowledge of electronics, aeronautics, or meteorology; in their prayer and relationship with God? Sometimes I think that every young person is a virtuoso-in-secret and that my role is to discover the virtuosity.

A friend of mine who is a high school principal once told me of his own experience as a teen. He said that at sixteen, if you knew almost everything about him but overlooked one key point, then in his mind you would have known nothing about him. You could have known where he lived, the names of everyone in his family, their birthdays, weight, test scores, grades, and so forth, without knowing him. At that age, he saw that all the externals of his life came to him from others, especially from his loving parents. Nothing was really his except one thing. One area was uniquely his, and he was astonished to see it developing in his life. It was this: If he had a basketball in his hands, no matter how many people were between him and the basket, he knew he could score. For him that knowledge symbolized the joy of life itself. Many teens take a similar joy in an emerging sense of their own sexuality.

As this example indicates, I am not concerned here merely with hobby-type competencies that young people develop, but rather with the emerging genius of a person's life, with its creative center. Any adult who is privileged to lead a young person to an appreciation of his or her own emerging gifts will also be given a loving place in that individual's memories. The namer-of-a-gift is in any person's life a special gift.

Ministry to Transformation

If ministry to gifts is one aspect of our fidelity to young people, then ministry to transformation is another and closely related aspect. I believe life is about transformation and that it tends to be continually confronted with a call for life-transforming change based on life-transforming decisions.[2] Erik Erikson and Daniel Levinson remind us that major steps in human growth take place by means of life crises, which confront people with major decisions. These occur during the teen years especially. For example, it is a decisive moment when a person emerges from the narcissism of childhood and realizes that other people do not exist for his or her own personal satisfaction and that they deserve our respect, even when they oppose our own self-interest. Most of us probably come to such a life-transforming realization many times in our lives. My hunch is that there is a first time of special insight that occurs sometime after puberty. This is just one example of what I am calling a moment of transformation. There are two key transformations we as teachers should be encouraging our youth towards: *the transformation of attention and the transformation of apathy.*

Something that has been plaguing all of us for some time, but in a largely unnoticed way, has been the manipulation of our attention away from significant matters and toward insignificant ones. Such manipulation is one of the worst aspects of the "shadow curriculum." At no other time in history have people been under such an assault on their senses from various electronic sources.[3] There are millions of people in the United States alone who are paid to figure out ways of catching our attention. All of us, young and old, are likely to have our attention caught by insignificant matters while we unwittingly ignore the significant. The great crisis of the human spirit in our time is deciding what matters are worth our attention. No spirituality is adequate to our world unless it deals with this issue. But focused attention on the proper matters results only from decision and discipline.

Today, multiple competing forces are struggling for the attention of young people. There are big profits from those who successfully manipulate the attention of youth. In the face of such intense competition, teachers striving for fidelity to young people need to propose the matters truly deserving of their attention. Let me outline some general directions:

First, we must help young people become aware of the subtle manipulation of their attention through various media. Such an awareness cannot be accomplished by diatribe or harangue, and should not be attempted through sermonizing. The key to awareness is analysis, but analysis calls for hard work. We need curriculum materials for helping youth develop an ability to understand how images work and to be alert to the manipulation that can come from them.

Second, we can lead our young people to become more aware of the social world. If I had two days with a group of young people, the first thing I might do is teach them how to read the newspaper for real news of the events and decisions that will affect them and their children. I would also help them to see that all news has been screened through a reporter's interpretation and also through editorial decisions. I would want them to become appropriately suspicious of one-sided reports—for example, to balance official statements with reports from less closely controlled sources.

Third, there are great issues staring the entire human race in the eyes, and our young people should be well-informed about them. I doubt that all these matters can be adequately covered in course work, partly because so many young people perceive the classroom as unreal and partly because courses tend to provide a single perspective rather than a holistic point of view. Nonviolence and disarmament, for example, may best be handled in a teach-in involving teachers from many disciplines, as well as student input. Such a teach-in might also be the best way of dealing with world hunger or with United States' policy in Central America. When an individual shows a preference for the needs of the poor and the weak and those whose human rights are violated, then that person's attention has been transformed in the direction of the gospel.

The Transformation of Apathy

At first glance the transformation of apathy seems almost the same as the transformation of attention. We commonly think of apathy as not caring, which is close to not paying attention. After all, what we do not care about, we do not pay attention to. However, apathy is derived from words denoting "not suffering." Apathy is a flight from suffering. An apathetic person is not willing to face the suffering involved in compassion and solidarity with those who suffer. So we deny suffering or turn away from it.

While it is true that the transformation of apathy in any of us is a transformation towards greater care, underlying this transformation is a decision not to turn away from those who suffer nor from the personal suffering involved in establishing solidarity with them. All know the difficulty of facing the sufferings of those we love most; everyone knows the temptation to run away as a defense against the intense suffering their suffering causes us. Those who never grow up develop a life stance of running away from such sufferings.

Although my example here is on a personal and interpersonal level, the transformation of apathy is a transformation of our willingness to face the social causes of suffering. Compassion beyond the interpersonal level calls for a special quality of imagination that can cross over into the experience of large groups of people, all of whom are individuals. This is hard: we feel anguish if we allow ourselves to think of how much suffering exists in the world. It is much easier to flip to the department store ads than to read the detailed piece about the ways the United States has supported dictatorship in Haiti for so many years, so that our government refuses refuge to those seeking to escape from it.

I am aware that what I have set forth here in the name of fidelity to youth are two difficult aspects of our ministry with young people: ministry to gifts and ministry to transformation. I am also aware of how much subtlety and attention one must bring to all these efforts, particularly to the effort to help youth face social suffering. The truth is that teaching in our day is about the challenging task of helping young people be emotionally and intellectually awake. Part of that task involves entering into the liberation of teens; acknowledging and supporting their emerging gifts; encouraging their commitment to their own freedom and to enlightened choice before mere comfort. Our fidelity to them calls them to their own fidelity to humankind.

---

[1]Some of the sources of these figures: Children's Defense Fund, *The Adolescent and Young Adult Fact Book* (Washington, DC: 1991); Cathy Simonelli-Chang, "Adolescent Suicide: A Library Guide," *Voice of Youth Advocates* (December 1981), pp. 19-20; Jim Jerome, "Catching Them Before Suicide," *The New York Times Magazine* 13 January 1979, pp. 30-33. See also, John Mack and Holly Hickler, *Vivienne: The Life and Suicide of an Adolescent Girl* (Boston: Little, Brown, 1981).

[2]For a good treatment see Donald Evans, *Struggle and Fulfillment* (New York: William Collins, 1979). See also Craig Dykstra, *Vision and Character: A Christian Educator's Alternative to Kohlberg* (New York: Paulist Press, 1981).

[3]See Susan Sontag, "The Habits of Consciousness: Interview by Roger Copeland," *Commonweal*, 108, no. 3 (13 February 1980): 86. See also George W. S. Trow, "Reflections: The Decline of Adulthood," *New Yorker,* 17 November 1980, pp. 63-171.

[4]The best analysis of apathy I have found is Dorothee Soelle, *Suffering* (Philadelphia: Fortress, 1975), esp. pp. 1-49. See also George Abbott White, "The Religion of the Privileged Ones: A Conversation with Robert Coles," *Cross Currents* 31, no. 1 (1981): 1-14.

Chapter 7
Young People, Weapons, Violence—and Alternatives

The original essay, written in the midst of working with the Youth for Peace project, was done at a time when a group of scientists estimated that U.S. and Soviet arsenals contained

> about 18,000 strategic thermonuclear warheads, with a... yield of 10,000 megatons [about 500,000 Hiroshimas], in addition to about 35,000 tactical and intermediate weapons. Yet not more than 500 to 2,000 strategic warheads would be enough to trigger a climactic catastrophe threatening the survival of the human race![1]

In these disheartening figures, I found frightening consequences for the youngest in the human family, whose futures were being put in ever greater jeopardy the further we move from the carefully justified misjudgment of August 1945. Contrary to popular perception, the nuclear threat has not disappeared with the collapse of the Soviet Union. I believe the horizon of violence we had been living in for most of this century persists, and further, that the nuclear threat has merely shifted, but in the process, has become more volatile, though less focused on. The gun once leveled at an intruder is now on an open gun rack, loaded, cocked, unattended to, and accessible. For those living in the U.S., which in 1990 was ranked internationally number one in weapons sales,[2] ample evidence supports this claim.[3] Even with the acclaimed Start II nuclear weapons treaty signed in 1993, the year 2003 will find both Russia and the U.S., each with approximately 3,500 nuclear warheads, enough to wipe all life off the planet. And this is after a 75% reduction in the size of the mutual arsenals. Unaffected by Start II are the nuclear weapons known to be owned by France, Britain, and China, and those not acknowledged in the arsenals of Israel, India, Pakistan.[4] That gun on the open rack is no toy.

Are young people aware of these dangers? At what ages do they become capable of being aware and at what levels of awareness? What are the effects of their awareness? What should the churches be doing in pastoral work with the young in the face of these issues? These questions will not be easily answered by those seeking fidelity to youth in the name of the gospel. If anything they have become more complex in the light of the collapse of the Soviet Union. Faithfulness in our day to both the human family and the community of followers of Jesus continues to demand the perceptual courage needed to stare long and hard at social evil and to discern its implications for action.[5] As for the questions listed above, adults have for almost a half-century colluded in avoiding the work needed to answer them. If anything, as adults' knowledge of the destructiveness of weaponry has become more extensive over the years, so has the moral lapse implicit in silence and inactivity become more serious. One researcher makes the following accusation.

> The fact that there is so little information available about how young people feel about nuclear issues that affect their lives so vitally suggests that we adults entered into a kind of compact with ourselves not to know. We suspect that the implications of what we are doing to the emotional development of our young are so horrifying that we would prefer to remain ignorant, for the veil of denial is easy enough to tear away once we set out to do so.[6]

There have, however, been a small group of researchers who have been quietly studying these questions and whose pioneering work eventually opened the way for a wider and more intense study of them starting about 1977. One of the earliest studies, Sybelle Escalona's "Children and the Threat of Nuclear War," is still cited often for its special insights.[7] After studying children's reactions to the 1963 Cuban Missile Crisis, she concluded that children apparently know a great deal more than we sometimes give them credit for. Children seem so absorbed in their games, their friends, their life at school, that it is hard to believe they pay much attention to grown-up problems. Yet even young children nearly always seem to know when something really matters to their elders. As soon as American families became concerned over issues of fallout, testing and shelter building, children also knew about these issues. Signs of their awareness turned up in the questions they asked and even in the games they played.[8]

Escalona reported that in 1961, when nuclear testing was stirring international concern, 98% of ten- and eleven-year-old children in one New York City school showed concern that there might not be a future world for them. Based on her studies, she concluded that "children four years old and up are aware of a danger to life. With greater or lesser understanding, they connect this danger with the language of nuclear war, fallout, Russia, radiation, H-bomb are all part of their vocabulary."[9] Particularly valuable in Escalona's report were her suggestions for parents in helping children have a continued sense of hope in the face of apocalyptic dread. A leitmotif threaded through Escalona's account is an assumption that a major problem for children and youth facing fears of apocalyptic destruction is the unwillingness of many parents and other adults to face these questions. In the minds of children especially, fearful matters that one is not allowed to talk about are perceived to be particularly bad or frightening. Silence only exacerbates fear.[10] When the loaded gun they spy on the gun rack is denied to exist or is claimed to be safe, their anxiety increases. On the other hand, children are helped simply by knowing that parents are thinking about such issues and have some definite ideas about them. Many later researchers have echoed Escalona's claim that young people draw strength from adults who do not shrink from the questions troubling youth and who communicate that life and human values are worth laboring for.[11]

The implications are obvious for those ministering to youth who may have decided, not always with full consciousness, that songs, hugs, and allusions to a loving God will absolve young people from worry about nuclear extinction. Some claim that the single most important force helping young people in their long struggle for maturity is the promise which the future holds, a promise that makes the process of growing up worthwhile.[12] However, when the future holds no promise but is itself perceived to be in jeopardy, youth move toward despair. One psychologist describes the sequence as follows.

> There are many...disappointments which a child must endure, such as the realization of being small or relatively weak, or that adult sexuality and childbearing are beyond a small girl's reach, or simply that there are other children who are smarter, better athletes, or in some respects more lovable. In adolescence, heightened sexual feeling, a desire for independence, and the development of new skills and capabilities are accompanied by the possibility of hurt and rebuff. At each stage of development, the child mitigates disappointments by looking ahead and building a vision of the future in which he or she may possess what cannot now be had, or in which it is possible to become what he or she is incapable of being now... But what happens to the ego ideal if society and its leaders are perceived cynically and the future itself is uncertain?...In such a context, impulsivity, a value system of "get it now," the hyperstimulation of drugs, and the proliferation of apocalyptic cults...seem to be natural developments.[13]

In spite of such descriptions of the psychological ramifications of life in the nuclear shadow, many persons working with youth continue to claim that youth are unaffected by the problem. To an extent, this claim has some merit, as explained by Escalona in 1965:

> Many teen-agers act as though they neither knew nor cared about a

threat to their future. When nuclear issues are mentioned, they turn them into a joke, or pay no attention, or become impatient. Some parents are concerned not because their adolescents worry too much about the danger but rather because they seem to show callous indifference.[14]

Researchers continue to pay close attention to why some young people seem to be aware and to care while others do not. Perhaps the closest scrutiny of the psychological processes affected by the threat of extinction has been done by Robert Jay Lifton, who developed the theory of psychic numbing: of becoming immune, at least on the conscious level, to matters so frightening they are more easily repressed than faced.[15] Ironically, a good summary of Lifton's later positions on this matter can be found in Escalona's early essay. She wrote,

whenever people deliberately close their eyes to facts, it means that they feel helpless and fatalistic. As one fifteen-year-old said, "Nothing can change things, no matter what you do." Refusal to acknowledge something unpleasant does not do away with it. Disturbing feelings still exist and undermine basic security, even when the adolescent does not admit these feelings to the self. Moreover, we know that a sense of being powerless over one's own fate is one of the most painful feelings in human experience. Somehow, the expressions of unconcern and disinterest do not ring true. They mask the underlying sense of apprehension.[16]

Until recently statements such as this have been truisms in the literature dealing with youth and apocalyptic destruction. Many working with youth still find this description useful, but others object to the assumption that young people are either consciously or unconsciously concerned and that if their concern is unconscious they have unwittingly repressed it in an unhealthy way. This serious objection was made by psychiatrist, Robert Coles in 1984, in a paper challenging researchers to become more rigorous in their methods and cautioning readers of such research not to overlook the nuances and qualifications found in the best studies.[17] In the United States, for example, Coles claimed that most studies have been biased toward certain populations, such as urban and middle and upper class young people, and that the studies reflect social and cultural concerns of these groups.[18] Further, many studies have dealt with very small populations, from which few generalizations could be drawn. Coles' warning reminds all that study of the effects of the nuclear threat on individuals and groups of various ages is at an introductory, almost primitive, stage. His caveat encourages youth ministers to approach their work with youth as an on-going experiment. Coles' reflections, however, should not intimidate those working with youth from striving to make tentative connections between the various aspects of the lives of young people and the spectre of nuclear annihilation. For example, consider the following fact. The United States is "the most violent in the industrialized world, with six million victims of violent crime a year, 23,000 of them murdered."[19] The data on how violence affects youth are readily available from multiple sources like the daily newspaper or the Annual Crime Report, published each August by the Justice Department. Occasional complications, such as *The Adolescent and Young Adult Fact Book,* published in 1991 by the Childrens' Defense Fund, bring together startling statistical facts. So much information is available, any person concerned for youth can easily find out the extent to which young people are growing up in a culture of violence.[20] If youth workers look into this matter, they may also be troubled at the possible connection between the production of weapons and the burgeoning cloud of personal violence under which youth in many countries seem to be living.

In choosing to address the apocalyptic threat, youth workers will have to search out appropriate strategies. They will face the continuing problem of the submerged consciousness of youth. For the child, social reality is taken for granted and unquestionable. Instead of being seen, the social system is the lens through which one sees and is thus invisible. In the expression, "submerged consciousness," the metaphor suggests fish swimming in water but unaware of the environment as water.[21] This submerged state continues into the teen years. Thus the problem of coming to understand social reality is complex and difficult, because it exists in the spaces between and among persons.

It is easy to describe what a person does, but to get at how the social reality influences that person's behavior one needs to know whose commands the person is following or whose norms the person has internalized and what sets of goals the person is trying, often unconsciously, to achieve. Social norms are most powerful when they dominate a person's life unawares. Social reality is like the underground transportation system of a large city. The system is essential but is for the most part invisible above ground. Even below ground, the passenger is aware of being on or in the system, but still cannot see it as a system or get much sense of its complexity. One's main experience of the system is of the immediate vehicle one is in. For the unthinking, that experience of a single vehicle represents the whole system. Even this analogy, however, has its limits, for it places the person within the system, whereas social reality also has an unfailing way of putting the system within the person.

The task of those who would be faithful to young people, and even more so of those who would invite them to discipleship, is to help them break out of childhood naivete about social reality and invite them to a lifetime journey to social awareness. This is a very gradual process.

Progress is as much marked by the asking of searching questions as by the giving of information. Compounding the frustration of slow progress is the arrival almost every year of a new generation of the socially naive, with whom the process must begin all over again. In working with the young on these matters, those who prefer exuberant enthusiasm and immediate response are certain to be disappointed. The process is low in exhilaration and high in gradualness. The see-judge-act approach of the Young Christian Worker/Student movements have practically collapsed in many countries. These movements were basically consciousness-raising movements involving the slow process of dialogue and questioning of reality tied to action.[22]

I fear the reason these movements have been replaced by more ebullient strategies is that the latter strategies seem to produce quicker results without requiring a commitment to formation for a lifetime.[23] What then are the possibilities of undertaking this task with young people? Except for Joseph Cardijn, the person who has most helped youth workers understand the nature of submerged consciousness and the possibilities of developing awareness has been Brazilian educator Paulo Freire.[24] He has shown how problem-posing strategies can help persons question taken-for-granted social arrangements and come to a fresh view, in which social reality no longer seems to be a divinely arranged, unquestionable entity. Instead it shows itself to be a series of human arrangements devised for the benefit of particular groups at particular times and for the disadvantage of other groups. Realizing that social reality is a human arrangement gives a person a valuable key with which to examine any and every aspect of it.

According to Freire, what helps many people understand social reality is oppression. By being challenged over and over again to face and question the injustice which they themselves are experiencing, even illiterate people can become knowledgeable and articulate about the causes and remedies of their oppression. In contrast, for young people in countries of the economic first world, their own comfortable situation seems to offer slight chance of moving them to a consciousness ready to question and critique. However, all young people in our day are oppressed by the climate of violence and its connection to weapons' production. A world bristling with weapons aimed at neighbors, ready to risk snuffing out forever the human experiment, cannot hide its own pathology. Even quite young children have been known to express simple insight: "This is crazy. Why would anyone want to blow up the whole world?" In a world where every city has now become Hiroshima, more sophisticated young people ask, "How has this situation come to pass? What are we trying to protect that is worth risking all of life?[25] It is as if smoke were billowing out of a tunnel of the underground transportation

system and calling attention not only to the system hidden there but to
the fact that something seriously wrong is happening there.

Would it were not so, but the fact remains that life in the nuclear
shadow offers immense possibilities to those interested in developing
social awareness among youth. Of course these possibilities must be
intelligently studied and pursued. For example, youth in the nations of
economic privilege face the danger that their concern for human survival
can become fixated at the level of concern for the survival, not so much
of the race, but of their own privileges. While self-interest is present in
everyone, the self-interest of the middle and upper classes in consumer
cultures has an edge of narcissistic self-preoccupation.[26] The unspoken
assumption that the survival of our class and of our nation is a special
concern because we are superior. This assumption must be directly challenged. As one probes the questions raised by nuclear weapons, ultimately one comes to issues of social justice. There is a clear relationship
between the arms race and economic exploitation.[27] To deal with questions of deterrence, as did the French and German bishops in their pastoral messages on peace in 1983,[28] as if these strategies affected only the
balance of power, is to ignore the economic root of the problem. In a
world that has since 1938, depended on the production of weapons to
maintain economic growth, Western nations would have had to invent
the Soviet Union if did it not exist, in order to legitimate the military focus
of their industrial system. Most of the above issues could be raised with
youth by non-religious persons of good will.

Followers of Jesus, however, bring a special perspective to these
issues. Nonviolence, based on the words and example of Jesus, appears
to be particularly important in a world characterized by fundamental patterns of violence. Many young people know neither Jesus' teachings on
this matter nor the tradition of nonviolence found, however obscurely, in
every period of the Christian era.[29] Making this teaching and tradition
accessible to youth could provide them with a valuable perspective from
which to examine modern life. Nonviolence offers young people who
espouse it a radical way of being in the world. A similar radical perspective is that of solidarity with victims. Once accepted as a way of following
the example of Jesus, solidarity with victims subverts the consumerist
culture of violence.[30] It involves paying attention to the concrete effects of
injustice and to the social evil causing such injustice.

Some strategies of so-called evangelization encourage young people to leap on the Jesus bandwagon, a form of middle-class self-affirmation. But solidarity with victims is a matter of transformative growth in
commitments that, by their very nature, caution against quick adoption.
For most young people, such slow growth needs the concrete example of
others trying to live in such solidarity. The Jesus such persons follow

bears no resemblance to the sweet Jesus of sentimental religious art, but neither is he as boring.

Life in the nuclear shadow inevitably forces us to re-examine accepted approaches to youth and to probe the implications for young people of the invitation to discipleship. Renewed youth ministry will be especially wary of fostering in young people the legitimation of political and social power that now holds all the world hostage to its greed. Unfortunately, not all adults working with youth in the economic first world have themselves thought through the implications of the nuclear threat for followers of Jesus. Those who have will find that the nuclear shadow calls for a special kind of spirituality for young people today, a spirituality of resistance to all that is inhuman in life.

Religious work with youth in the past has put far more focus and stress on gaining the compliance of young people than on encouraging their resistance. One could argue that the greatest horrors of the twentieth century have come about by means of too much obedience, for one example, the obedience of males holding guns to the commands of officers. When disobedience in the name of humanity was called for, it was not chosen. So one who proposes a spirituality of resistance for youth is not living in an ivory tower but is perhaps well aware of the debris of our century. Of course compliance and resistance are related: Knowing what to resist is the other side of knowing what to assist. If youth begin to resist militarism and violence, greed and self-preoccupation, and patterns of thought and action that reduce other people to objects, then perhaps they can also assist in building solidarity across sexual, class, and national barriers.

There are obvious problems in the proposals made here. They raise many questions about the consciousness of adult Christians today and about the kind of church that deserves the attention of youth. Also, solidarity with victims, nonviolence, and a spirituality of resistance will not appeal to all young people. Most likely, such a program will be embraced only partially and gradually, but such is the way of growth, not only for youth but for disciples of all ages. Those who work with youth can unwittingly adopt a pied piper approach to the young, marching them along to the sound of a sweet tune. In the fairy tale of that name, however, the pied piper was basically one who betrayed the children who followed him. Finally, the spirituality for youth facing the humanly created apocalypse is a spirituality of hope, which is to be worked out in the face of its opposite, despair.[31]

There is no true Christian hope that has not looked evil in the eye, chosen to resist, and put the final victory in the hands of a loving God. Such was the adult hope that Jesus embodied. It is the only form of hope appropriate for young people living in the nuclear shadow.

[1]Theodore Draper, "Nuclear Temptations," *New York Review of Books*, 18 January 1984, p. 48.

[2]Robert Pears, "U.S. Ranked No. 1 in Weapons Sales," *The New York Times* (11 August 1991): 10. The study ranking the U.S. this was by done by the Congressional Research Service, a research arm of the Library of Congress.

[3]Some information sources: Center for Defense Information, *The Defense Monitor*, "We Arm the World," 20:4 (1991); "Stopping the Spread of Nuclear Weapons: Still Time to Act," 21:3 (1992); "Arming Dictators," 21:5 (1992); "World at War—1992," 21:6 (1992). J. Bryan Hehir, "The Proliferation Problem," *Commonweal* (25 October 1991): 598-599; Amata Miller, IHM, "Turning Swords to Plowshares: Necessity, Challenge and Opportunity," *Blueprint for Social Justice* 45:5 (January 1992).

[4]See, Thomas L. Friedman, "Beyond Start II: A New Level of Instability," *The New York Times*, 10 January 1993, pp. E1, E3. See, too, on p. E3 of this report the extensive overview of the transfer of nuclear and missile technology among nations since 1990.

[5]"...moral courage has its source in...identification through one's sensitivity with the suffering of one's fellow human beings. I am tempted to call this `perceptual courage' because it depends on one's capacity to perceive, to let oneself see the suffering of other people. If we let ourselves experience the evil, we will be forced to do something about it" (Rollo May, *The Courage to Create* [New York: Bantam, 1976], p. 8).

[6]William Beardslee and John Mack, "The Impact on Children and Adolescents of Nuclear Developments," in Rita Rogers et al., *Psychosocial Aspects of Nuclear Developments, Task Force Report 20* (Washington, D.C.: American Psychiatric Assn., 1982), p. 91.

[7]Sibylle Escalona, "Children and the Threat of Nuclear War" in *Behavioral Science and Human Survival*, ed. Milton Schwebel (Palo Alto, Calif: Behavioral Science Press, 1965), pp. 3-24.

[8]Ibid.

[9]Ibid., pp. 4-5.

[10]Ibid., p. 5.

[11]Ibid., p. 11.

[12]Ibid., p. 15.

[13]Beardslee and Mack, p 90.

[14]Escalona, p. 19.

[15]See Robert Jay Lifton, "Beyond Nuclear Numbing," *Teachers College Record* 84, no. 1 (1982): 15-29, and "The Psychic Toll of the Nuclear Age," *The New York Times Magazine,* 26 September 1982, 52ff.

[16]Escalona, pp. 19-20.

[17]Robert Coles, "Children and the Nuclear Bomb," in *The Moral Life of Children* (Boston: Atlantic-Little Brown, 1985).

[18]Coles' essay includes a useful review of this research literature, as does the essay of Beardslee and Mack, *Nuclear Developments*, pp. 64-73.

[19]Boyce Rensberger, "Study of U.S. Violence Urges Remedies," The Washington *Post* (November 13, 1992). This articles announces the encyclopedic report issued by the National Research Council, the working arm of the National Academy of Sciences.

[20]See Christina Robb, "Are We Hooked on Media Violence?" Boston *Globe* (July 8, 1991), pp. 27, 30. In the final chapter of this book, I offer more sources and facts about the climate of violence in which our young people live.

[21]The notion of submerged consciousness is found in Paulo Freire, "Cultural Action and Conscientization," *Harvard Educational Review* 40, no. 3 (1970): 452-477. It has been reprinted as Chapter 7 in Paulo Freire, *The Politics of Education* (South Hadley, Mass.: Bergin and Garvey, 1985), pp. 67-96.

[22]See, Joseph Cardijn, *Laymen into Action* [Trans. by Anne Heggie] (London: Geoffrey Chapman, 1964).

[23]The ebullient strategies I have in mind are found in weekends stressing religious self-affirmation, usually in apolitical, class-stratified groups of young people. Chapter 11 of this book is a critique of these weekends. An important essay providing background toward a critique is Gregory Baum, "Theology Questions Psychiatry," *The Ecumenist* 20:4 (May-June, 1982): 55-59.

[24]See *Pedagogy of the Oppressed* (New York: Herder and Herder, 1970) and *Education for Critical Consciousness* (New York: Seabury, 1973).

[25]For an account of how statespersons, negotiators, and technicians alike have drifted away from these fundamental questions, see Thomas Powers, "What Is It About?" *Atlantic Monthly*, January 1984: 35-55.

[26]See Dorothee Soelle, "The Need for Liberation in a Consumerist Society" in *The Challenge of Liberation Theology*, ed. Brian Mahan and L. Dale Richesin (New York: Orbis, 1981), pp. 4-16.

[27]See Bishop Roger Mahony, "Adverse Effects of the Arms Race in the Third World," *Origins* 14, no. 4 (7 June 1984): 55-60.

[28]About the same time in 1983, the episcopal conferences of the United States, France, Germany, Belgium, the Netherlands, and Japan issued pastoral statements on peace. These messages—with the exception of that of the Japanese bishops—tend to overlook the suffering caused in the Southern Hemisphere by the arms race of nations of the North. The East-West ideological polarity masks the underlying North-South polarity, which is economic and at root a question of justice rather than of creed. In comparing these pastoral statements, note how the Japanese bishops frame their thoughts with attention to the economic injustice of the arms race. Young

people will need the economic critique in order to fully assess the ideological conflict. The texts of the pastorals of the United States and French bishops are in *Origins*, vol. 13 (1983); the texts of the others can all be found in *La Documentation Catholique* (1983), nos. 1846 and 1863.

[29]For a scholarly treatment, see Jean-Michel Hornus, *It Is Not Lawful for Me to Fight: Early Christian Attitudes Toward War, Violence and the State* (Scottsdale, Penn.: Herald, 1980.

[30]Youth workers would do well to study and draw out the implications for their ministry of the following work: Matthew L. Lamb, *Solidarity with Victims: Toward a Theology of Social Transformation* (New York: Crossroads, 1982).

[31]A very important book about facing despair, though not written from a Christian perspective is: Joanna Rogers Macy, *Despair and Personal Power in the Nuclear Age* (Philadelphia: New Society, 1983).

Chapter 8
A Spirituality of Reversibility

A properly grounded youth ministry approaches its work well-focused on the social system in which youth are embedded. This chapter looks at young people from the angle of what that social system does to their spirits, with an eye to offering a spirituality that might begin to reverse the negative aspects of their life condition.

As a way of looking at the situation of youth, I wish to begin with a poem, because poetry has a way of making accessible truths that sometimes cannot be gotten at with statistical data. The poem "At Peace, At Rest," is by Joyce Carol Oates,[1] a writer whose work has paid a fair amount of attention to young people. It provides insight into some important aspects of the lives of youth today.

AT PEACE, AT REST
Stranded amiably on an island
of pavement by the drugstore
amid the crumpled wrappers and cigarette butts

in the 87° heat
there are three boys and two girls
sitting with their backs to the wall
arms linked loose about their knees
untalking
untroubled

in blue jeans and shapeless shirts
one boy in a purple jacket, unzipped
they sit hunched over their knees
blinking in the sunshine
not talking
not waiting

The manager of the drugstore looks out
and ten minutes later looks out again
the children are peaceful they are no trouble
they are watching traffic
at one o'clock they are still there

they are still there
another boy has joined them
fourteen years old and yawning and heavy-headed

half smiling at the traffic
he nudges one of the girls
they talk briefly they are old friends
they light cigarettes together
they stare at the traffic
they are silent

They are not waiting
they are not expecting anything
Every holiday has arrived every package torn open

It is here, it is now
No trouble
At rest.

What feeling do we get from the poem? What is the significance of the "crumpled wrappers," the "cigarette butts," "the drugstore," or the "purple jacket, unzipped?" I suggest that at least in part the poem reflects three key elements missing in the lives of the young people it describes and in all young people today: a lack of expectations, of attention, and of connectedness. The lack of expectations is clearly suggested in the text. These boys and girls are not waiting for anyone, although others may join them if they like. These young people are also not going anywhere, have no desire to go anywhere, as they sit watching others moving in the traffic. Oates' juxtaposition of traffic movement with human immobility strongly suggests a lack of purpose. Here we find no expectations and no longing. Everything has already come to pass, "every package" is already "torn open."

Lack of attention is the second missing element. Even while "watching" the traffic, they do not really pay attention. They do not even pay attention to each other, except very briefly, as when the newcomer nudges and speaks a few words to the girl he knows. Ordinarily when we speak of people not paying attention, we mean that they are not attending to what we want them to pay attention to. Usually the inattentive ones are daydreaming—at least that is what we call it when they are attending to something more personally interesting than what we are saying. Possibly the correct term here is "alternate attention," because there is attention to something, though not to our agenda. However, the context of this poem suggests a total lack of attention to anything, a sort of half sleep. Note how tied to their lack of attentiveness is their peaceful behavior. They are not causing trouble. If the poet is troubled by the scene she describes, could she be most troubled by this nontrouble? The nervous drugstore manager is possibly looking for some trouble but finds none. The young people here appear to be simply minding their own business.

Finally, the poem depicts a lack of connectedness: they are not paying attention to one another. We find here a concrete example of proximity replacing communion and communication. True, the seven are stranded on an island together, sitting as a group, but the context suggests almost no interaction, as if each were on a separate island.

Are young people in our time really like the young people Joyce Carol Oates describes? Yes and no. Surely many of us have seen similar scenes of complete passivity. Some of us may remember that in their own youth such times provided a gentle way of relaxing from tension and trouble. On the other hand, I have never met young people who could sustain such passivity for very long. Most probably the poem describes an interlude or a prelude to later, perhaps frantic, activity. We can easily imagine these young people leaping to their feet to dash off madly through the traffic, laughing and talking. So the poem is true and not true. Young people exhibit these qualities, but not continuously. However, from a symbolic point of view, the poem is quite true and presents us with a most suggestive image of youth in our time. Let us look at each of these three missing elements more closely.

Lack of Expectations

Young people have serious questions about how long they will survive into the future. Those who care about young people need to pay careful attention to such questions. In 1982 Beardslee and Mack summarized their own research with young people the following way.

> Results of our questionnaire survey strongly suggest that... [young people] are deeply disturbed about the threats of nuclear war and the risks of nuclear power, while they also recognize possible benefits from nuclear power and nuclear weapons.... Our strongest finding, we feel, is a general unquiet or uneasiness about the future and about the present nature of nuclear weapons and nuclear power. There is a particular uncertainty and fear about nuclear war or the limiting of such a war should it occur, and the possibilities of survival.[2]

This research-based conclusion may be especially helpful for the way it explains some of the phenomena of youth today: their growing willingness to take their own lives and the growth of self-destructive behavior such as drug and alcohol abuse, violence, and reckless driving.[3] Robert Jay Lifton suggests that both the demand for instant gratification among some young people and the rush of others for the safest and best-paying jobs are related to a lack of expectations.[4]

The fundamental importance of being able to presuppose a future was brought home to me during a weekend on peacemaking, when a woman told me the following story. Her son, now twenty-five, had been diagnosed at ten as having an incurable bone cancer. Although never told the true scope of his problem, he must have intuited it. He had always been a superb student, but shortly after his illness was discovered he lost almost all interest in school work. After a year and a half of failing grades, his mother happened to mention the problem to the son's doctor. The doctor sided strongly with the boy. "What do you expect?" he asked the mother. "Think about it from his perspective. Why should he study and work at school when he doesn't see that he has a future? When and if he ever sees that he does have a future, his grades will improve." And that was exactly what happened. It took about five years of treatment to heal his cancer and two more to convince all that he was in permanent remission. Only then did his school work begin to improve. His mother was quite proud that he had graduated from college with honors.

Lack of Attention

Chapter Four introduced this problem and its connection with television. Empirical research on televiewing shows that, even with respect to eye movements, people watching television remain inactive and highly passive. However, to read one must make rapid eye movements, a different level of activity entirely. Researchers are now theorizing that people who watch a lot of television tend to read poorly because they are not accustomed to the physical alertness required for reading. Children who watch television a lot display a high level of passivity in all their activities.[5] Paying attention, on the other hand, involves some degree of concentration and activity. Even what I have described as "alternate attention" could be the result of a lack of discipline in focusing on a matter at hand. Somewhat ironically, the problem of inattention is stimulating more and more attention in educators, partly because of cross-cultural studies of first and fifth graders in three different countries.[6] These studies showed that children in the United States paid significantly less attention in class and did less reading outside of class than their counterparts in other countries. In an interview, essayist Susan Sontag noted that many people are now finding more and more things difficult and finding that they do not have the energy to cope with them.

Asked what caused this loss of energy, she replied, "For one thing, the acceptance of television, the mentality and kind of attention that is given television. The condition of our attention, the condition of our serious- ness has been progressively altered.... What's actually happening is that it's destroying our ability to concentrate and pay attention."[7] What Sontag had noticed about adults surely applies to youth.

Lack of Connectedness

The missing elements suggested in Oates' drugstore loungers are not those of young people alone. They are also lacking in our society, as many commentators have pointed out. Sociologist Robert Bellah has noted the danger in the strong strain of individualism that has character- ized the United States since its early days. Long ago, Alexis de Tocqueville had warned that United States citizens tended to withdraw from the mass of people into the smaller circle of family and friends, leaving the greater society to look after itself. Such an attitude, he warned, would make the United States vulnerable to tyranny that would succeed by limiting individual activity to purely private pursuits.[8]

According to Bellah and colleagues, this individualism committed to the self rather than to the common good has reached a particularly intense point of development in our day. In a series of interviews with professional people, Bellah and his colleagues found that they tended to be concerned only with short-term, private, and individual goals.[9] We can find more obvious examples in the selfish, sometimes smiling, some- times snarling, characters who people the nighttime soaps.

We should not be surprised that such individualism is a growing characteristic of our young people. For years now reports on college enrollments and on the attitudes of incoming first-year college students have showed that more and more students were picking their college fields solely in terms of quick financial payoff.[10] College administrators have commented: "We are seeing more students who want to do well [financially] and do it right away"; "Young people are looking for short- term payoffs"; and "Students are more enticed by the chance to move quickly into fields like computer science and engineering without spend- ing time and money to prepare for a profession that requires an addition- al degree." After discussing these three lacks with youth workers, I have found the one they are most concerned about is lack of connectedness.

The Question of Reversibility

Can anything be done about the situation of youth as presented in Oates' poem? Thomas Merton once wrote that the greatest of human spiritual needs is the need to be delivered from the evil and falsity in one-self and in one's society, and that tyranny seeks to convince people that this evil is of its very nature unshakeable. "Modern tyrannies have all explicitly or implicitly in one way or another emphasized the irreversibili-ty of evil in order to build their power upon it."[11]

If this situation is reversible, it will not happen by accident or chance. The forces of social conditioning are so subtle and so powerful—even massive, because of the way they mesh one with the other—that they are reversible only through the sustained effort of a community of people proposing in a loving way a different set of values and a different way of living from that of the prevailing culture. Those seeking the courage to face this task will do well to remember that the entire thrust of the *ekklesia* (the assembly of the followers of Jesus) is that evil is not irreversible. The reversibility of evil and injustice is a central element in the symbol of the resurrection. Jesus died a criminalized, unjust death, and the Father raised him up as a living spirit, thus giving the lie to the suggestion that injustice will have the last word. Life in an *ekklesia* living this insight will itself be a reversal of youth's situation as found in our poem.

Notice how the notion of the kingdom or reign of God, once under-stood, accepted, and lived, actually runs counter to all three lacks. Those who await the kingdom, the new time of justice when people act accord-ing to God's wishes, are filled with expectations. Again and again, Jesus' parables stress the theme of eager anticipation: the bridegroom is com-ing; the master is returning; the bread is rising; the weeds will eventually be sorted from the wheat, and so forth. These are not passive expecta-tions but working expectations fleshed out in actions that seek to initiate the new time. Instead of "every package torn open," we have the oppo-site in Jesus' promise, "Behold, I make all things new."

The imagery of the kingdom also reverses the lack of attention. Because the new times are at hand, we must pay attention to the signs of the times and be ready to understand what is happening. Many of the New Testament's kingdom parables also have a theme of paying atten-tion. The deepest failure of the young women awaiting the bridegroom was not in their waiting but in the poor quality of the attention they paid during their waiting. They forgot about the oil for their lamps. Similarly in the great parable of the last judgment, not all were paying proper atten-tion. They had not realized that attending to the poor and the suffering was in fact a way of attending to God. The *ekklesia* is the community of focused attention, and catechesis is its attention therapy. Focused atten-tion is its gift to youth.

Similarly, the *ekklesia* is also the place of connectedness, not only among those in the community but in its understanding of the sisterhood and brotherhood of all in the spirit of Jesus. This is a connectedness across national barriers and across the barriers separating person from person. The New Testament highlights human connectedness, and the ekklesia is meant to embody it. It espouses solidarity with victims and risk-taking toward solidarity. When local churches have moved beyond middle-class self-affirmation and the sharp individualism fostered by consumerism, then young people will have a space where the quest for unity can be lived out.

There are still more possibilities. Young people may come to understand that we live in a new time facing new dilemmas no longer resolvable through old answers. In fact, many young people instinctively sense the wisdom, once it is proposed to them, of recognizing that in our world we need new ways of being together, of sharing human goals across national boundaries. If Johannes Metz is correct that in our time grace "is the ability to interrupt, to stop... not having to go on living as before,"[12] then this is a grace that can take strong root in the young. According to Metz, part of this grace involves coming to see ourselves through the eyes of our victims. I have found that more young people than adults are willing to adopt such a way of seeing themselves.

One could say that reversing the situation depicted in "At Peace, At Rest" involves an integrated spirituality for youth, a spirituality of expectation, of attentiveness, and of connectedness—and underlying them all, a commitment to the reversibility of evil with all the strategies of resistance such a commitment will involve. Perhaps here there is an agenda for youth ministry that will take a long time to exhaust.

---

[1]Joyce Carol Oates, *Women Whose Lives Are Food; Men Whose Lives Are Money* (Baton Rouge: Louisiana State University Press, 1978), p. 61.

[2]William Beardslee and John Mack, "The Impact on Children and Adolescents of Nuclear Development," in Rita Rogers et al., *Psychological Aspects of Nuclear Developments, Task Force Report 20* (Washington, D.C.: American Psychiatric Assn., 1982), pp. 88-89.

[3]A source of statistical data on youth, with some useful crosscultural comparisons, will supplement the data available from the US. Census Bureau. This source is Minister of State for Youth, *Youth/Jeunesse: A New Statistical Perspective on Youth in Canada* (Hull, Quebec: Public Affairs Branch, 1984).

[4]Robert Jay Lifton, "The Psychic Toll of the Nuclear Age," *The New York Times Magazine*, 26 September 1982, pp. 52 ff. See also R.J.Lifton and R. Falk, Indefensible Weapons (New York: Basic Books, 1982), p. 73.

[5]See Marie Wynn, *The Plug-in Drug* (New York: Bantam, 1978), pp. 54-72.

[6]Edward Fiske, "U.S. Pupils Lag from Grade 1," *The New York Times,* 17

June 1984, pp. A1 and A30.

[7]"The Habits of Consciousness: Interview with Susan Sontag," *Commonweal* 108 no. 3 (13 February 1980): 86.

[8]Robert N. Bellah, "Religion and Power in America Today," *Commonweal*, 3 December 1982, pp. 650-55.

[9]See Robert N. Bellah, et al., *Habits of the Heart: Individualism and Commitment in American Life* (Berkeley and Los Angeles: University of California Press, 1985).

[10]See, Gene I. Maeroff, "Enrollment in Professional School Declining," *The New York Times*, 2 October 1984, pp. A1 and A50.

[11]Thomas Merton, *Gandhi on Nonviolence* (New York: New Directions, 1964), p. 13.

[12]Johannes Metz, "Towards the Second Reformation," *Cross Currents* 31:1 (Spring 1981): 85-98, at 94.

Chapter 9
Critical Consciousness Toward Peacemaking

This chapter deals with conscription and military service. I wish to set out some of the background thinking that led me to work with others to develop training programs for youth concerned with peacemaking and nonviolence. Every time I have shared these ideas with others, they have met with either fervent agreement or disagreement but never with yawns. For some years before initiating the Youth for Peace program, when I examined the agenda of the churches for youth, I found not a blessed rage for God or a blessed rage for truth, but a rage for doctrinal fixity and certitude. I saw, and continue to see, a rush to indoctrinate young people with sure and final answers, a kind of assault on doubt, a prohibition of tentativeness and of lingering questions. Even when not fully overt, this tendency to indoctrinate remains part of what the churches want for youth. I see in this only half the loaf of the church's doctrinal nourishment.

The other half of the community's self-understanding is marked by its hundreds of lingering questions and its many fragments of wisdom still unconnected to our current situation. For example, the church's unfinished, struggling search for credibility and integrity is not often held up to young people as unspoken permission to pursue their own integrity and their own completeness. Perhaps some leaders are not comfortable with this side of ecclesial life. With this half of the church's life hidden from them, the young are often subjected to moral injunctions about sexuality, overstatements of sacramental efficacy, and understatements of the Christian teaching on social justice. These are the real lapses in the doctrinal teaching offered young people.

Now suppose that all those dealing with youth started paying attention to a new agenda and began calling young people to face a different set of concerns? Suppose we worked to lead young people to a critical consciousness of how the world works? Suppose at the same time we invited youth to embrace the great messianic vision of God's reign of peace and justice? Suppose we empowered young people to deal with the great questions of our day and to speak out on these matters with the fresh insight young people sometimes have? Such action would tie what Christians believe to the way they are in the world and would open up forms of response to the gospel that are beyond the private sphere.

Can the dreams and visions of young people struggling for fidelity to the gospel become points of orientation to the elders in the community? More basically, can we offer them a Christianity they can enter into, as a historically-rooted effort to struggle for justice and to come to grips with the great causes of our time? Can we move away from programs of sacramental blackmail ("Come to our classes or you won't be confirmed") and respond to those ready to go deeper with us in facing the challenge the gospel offers us all today? Can we move from all-encompassing programs and instead develop small groups in which those who are ready to take a step together can begin their walk toward fidelity to Jesus' way?

If someone asked me to name the most important youth ministry issues today, I would not respond with many of the matters—important as they may be—that are usually set forth: friendship, sex education, faith development, evangelization, and so forth. Instead of these, I would select the issue of access. To what issues and opportunities do we give youth access? To what kinds of information do we give them access? In the United States today, young people have easy access to the following trivia: to money and to the purchase of status, especially through clothes; to images being retailed specifically to them through television, films, and popular music; to sexual stimulation from many sources; and to political platitudes, misinformation, and even lies through the media. These are the matters they pay most attention to, because access focuses attention. There is an agenda here for young people, though it is not such a savory agenda, at least not in gospel terms. I select access as the key youth ministry issue because it helps us to get to the important religious question of youth-in-culture.

The significance (and the dangers) of access to agenda, which is the agenda of the marketeers, is apparent when one asks to what vital matters young people do not have access.[1] In general they do not have access to critical viewpoints that encourage them to be skeptical about society's agenda for them—a society that exploits them in the pursuit of profits at the same time that it is quite cynical about their future. In most youth ministry literature, one finds little attention to the matter of fostering a critical consciousness, which asks without ceasing, "Who profits from this arrangement?" "In whose best interests is this way of doing things?" To ask such questions does not mean that one is automatically disrespectful of authority. Instead it means knowing one is grown-up enough to have the right to question and to expect the person in authority to have the courtesy to respond. Without these questions there is not even a beginning of a spirituality of reversibility.

Ironically, in North America today, one of the most visible groups questioning the wisdom of official governmental policies and even the good faith of official reports is to be found among the bishops. Certain bishops are leading the way in encouraging religious people to question authority, resist oppression, and disobey the law when the law conflicts with conscience. Here I am referring not only to sections on conscience in the U.S. Roman Catholic bishops' pastoral on peace but to other statements of various denominations that clearly contradict official positions of the United States government.[2] In Canada, the 1984 Roman Catholic bishops' pastoral letter on economics, "Ethical Choices and Political Challenges,"[3] caused a furor among investors because its radical principles contradicted dominant business practices. Although the same sort of questioning is going on among some lay people in the North American churches, it is unclear how many of those working with youth in these churches are encouraging young people to follow the bishops' lead.

A radical question that any Christian has a right to ask but that a young Christian may have an obligation to ask has to do with conscription into the military. At the moment I write about this issue, conscription is not longer practiced in the U.S., but the apparatus for re-activating conscription is, in the form of registration for the draft. To understand how important the apparatus appears to those who keep it in place, one must consider that the stated penalties for *not registering* are a $10,000 fine and ten years' imprisonment. To put these penalties in perspective one would have to examine the roster of crimes specifying punishments of this order.

This matter represents a classic case of how society views its young. Conscription, whether in actual use or in readiness for future use, presupposes that the life plans and careers of young people can be postponed in a way that no other age group's can. Youth are expendable because they have not yet had significant access to economic power and because, as a group, they tend both to be so little informed and to have so little solidarity, that they cannot speak effectively to the powers of government.

Conscription presupposes that the brutalization of the human spirit called "basic training" is appropriate for the young. In basic training the kind of domestication and predictability suitable to an animal is imposed on a human being. Here we have schooling in unquestioning obedience, in the ways of killing, and in the technology of death. We need only remember that the great horrors of our century have been committed by males wearing military uniforms, all of whom were schooled in basic training. That training was geared to make of them a fighting machine, with mechanization overriding humanization. Although basic training

ends after a certain number of weeks, the attitudes and patterns of
behavior and speech that it imposes last a lifetime for many. In *The
Long Revolution*, Raymond Williams has explained this imprinting in a
compelling way.

> One very powerful model [providing an image of society]... has of
> course been the modern army, which with conscription extended itself to
> the sense of a whole society. Here the stress on rank, on corporate spirit,
> and on single purpose has powerfully taught successive generations a
> way of thinking about relationships that has perhaps gone much deeper
> than we know. When we think how many individuals, in our century,
> have passed through this model, usually in periods of great emotional
> stress, the effect is hardly surprising. It is remarkable how many social
> organizations, with quite general and ordinary social purposes (even of a
> pacifist, reforming or free educational kind) speak of "recruiting" mem-
> bers, and of their "rank and file."... Middle class people speak of their
> ordinary holidays as "leave".... It is impossible to watch men in actual
> relationships, in the typical modern industrial or commercial organiza-
> tion, or in an ordinary government or local authority service, without see-
> ing this odd image of a medieval court (as in the graded sitting of offi-
> cials round a committee table) blended with a modern army unit (partic-
> ular tones of voice and stiffenings of the body)[4]

That side of the church's life that apes the chains of command and
positional hierarchies of military life is a matter beyond my scope here.
However, where allegiance to the gospel is a basic life value, a person will
tend to question all arrangements that run counter to it. The more radical
youth ministry becomes in its allegiance to discipleship, the more critical
questions it raises among youth about military arrangements.

Once again, the critical question is: Who profits from these
arrangements? Young people should know that a 1980s Yankelovitch
poll showed that those most in favor of renewal of the draft were over
thirty years old, with those farthest away from draft age most in favor of
it. If one proposed a new draft in which no one could be drafted who was
under fifty years old or earning less than fifty thousand dollars a year,
one might indeed find the answer to the critical "who profits" question.

Such a system should not be dismissed out of hand. It would
assure young people the chance to become more established
economically and to raise families before disrupting their lives. It would
force those who had achieved professional success to step aside and
allow younger persons access to key leadership roles and to better paying jobs. Society could better afford loss of life among over-fifty soldiers,
because they would already have had an opportunity to carry out some
of their basic life tasks. Besides all of which, the new draftees would have

a greater stake in any war fought to protect their privileges. Of course, there never will be a new draft in this sense, so long as the elders of the nation continue to view youth as so thoroughly expendable.

On occasions when I shared this scheme in large-group sessions on youth ministry, listeners have jumped to their feet and screamed at me, so enraged have they become. Possibly their rage would have been lessened had they known that Nathaniel Hawthorne offered a similar idea at the time of the U.S. Civil War. He wrote,

> It is a pity that old men grow unfit for war, not only by their incapacity for new ideas, but by the peaceful and unadventurous tendencies that gradually possess them.... It is a pity; because it would be such an economy of human existence if time-stricken people... could snatch from their juniors the exclusive privilege of carrying on the war. In case of death upon the battlefield, how unequal would be the comparative sacrifice. On one part, a few unenjoyable years, the little remnant of a life grown torpid; on the other, the many fervent summers of manhood in its spring and prime, with all that they include of possible benefit to mankind....
>
> If I had the ordering of these matters, fifty should be the tenderest at which a recruit might be accepted for training [emphasis added]; at fifty-five or sixty I would consider him eligible for most kinds of military duty and exposure... As a general rule these venerable combatants should have the preference for all dangerous and honorable service in the order of their seniority, with a distinction in favor of those whose infirmities might render their lives less worth the keeping.[5]

Notice how Hawthorne's position radically questions the assumptions about military service current in his day, and thus represents a stance of critical thinking.

Through critical consciousness, taken-for-granted procedures come under intense scrutiny. Young people may come to see that military service is false empowerment. It seems real, because they are given real weapons and taught to use them. But the self-actualization offered is that of killers. They are given the false status of the military uniform and the pseudo-status of military rank,[6] obscuring the fact that they have become digits, pawns, cogs in a fighting machine. The true symbol of military service is found in the serial number stamped on metal, which one wears as a collar around one's neck, in order to identify one's corpse or bones after death. This symbol is appropriately called a dog tag and was perhaps originally so named by someone who saw the correlation between the domestication of animals and that of military personnel.

In the militarization of youth, of special interest is the way one generation which has submitted to military life is so quick to impose it on the next. The idea seems to be: We submitted to this indignity, and so must you. This system will help you become "real men" as it did us. It will measure for you as it did for us the depth of your dedication to such values as patriotism, freedom, and courage. It will offer your generation a place in history as it did ours. If you come back from war physically whole, you can tell tales of glory as we do, and you too can demand of the young the same servitude. And if you return in living pieces, we will store you decently in a comfortable-enough facility where you will be spared the embarrassment of normal society.

If young people need access to critical standpoints, they also need access to solidarity, to the opportunity of joining one another in fostering sane human values. Not many will otherwise be able to resist social pressures toward militarism. At present young people have the trivial solidarity of spectator sports or of rock concerts. But even in a cheering group of tens of thousands, this solidarity is mute and powerless. Fashion in clothing is another form of insignificant solidarity. A review of such fashion magazines as *Cosmopolitan* shows that they offer readers not individuality but individualism—a focus on the self and a preoccupation with appearances. Indeed, fashion may be the ultimate in a depoliticized, totally predictable, pseudo-solidarity.

If those working with youth make the effort to offer them critical standpoints, they will find the young applying these standpoints to a wide range of social practices. A good example of how such critical thinking is almost naturally extended was given me by a young military officer, with whom I had shared my critique of military servitude. He replied with the following defense which insightfully points to the collusion of other structures in keeping the military machine going. He said (and I use the emphasis of his spoken words): "Don't ever forget that those soldiers went to *your* schools and learned *your* religion and *your* morality, and were given their mandate by civilians whom *you* elected, civilians from the highest educational levels and who are sworn to uphold the highest ethical norms." He clearly understood the implications of the critique. Would that teachers and others working with young people understood these connections as well as he did.

As I have stated so often in this book, the weapons industry with the extensive human ills it produces, including environmental deterioration, is the place where many of the ills of our time intersect and become visible. On these ills, society needs to hear the voice of its young, best heard through forms of solidarity that are competent, well-informed, and articulate. I expect to find more sanity—and certainly a greater commitment to gospel values—among Christian youth than among the Pentagon planners of the Great Death. When young people in one voice proclaim, "It is our future and our children's and we don't want to give you a final say in it," we may have stepped away from the insane master-plans of middle-aged and old men possessed of a diabolical disregard for the future.

With the exception of the Young Christian Students and the Young Christian Workers, whose unfortunate decline I mentioned earlier, there are few church-based youth groups in North America dealing specifically with consciousness-raising and action-for-change. Most youth groups are focused on the important but limited issues of friendship and community-building. Those who organized Youth for Peace have sought to provide an organization where those young people who see the need for action for peace can find their collective voice. The Youth for Peace training weekends were designed to launch them on their way to a lifetime of questioning from a gospel standpoint. In my view the so-called New World Order does not diminish the need for such efforts; it accentuates that need.

---

[1]One of the reasons I was so pleased with the title, *Access Guides to Youth Ministry*, for the series of youth ministry resource books being put together by the Center for Youth Ministry Development was precisely their highlighting *access* as a key youth ministry matter.

[2]See, for example, "U.S. Bishops' Statement on Central America," *Origins* 11, no. 25 (3 December 1981): 393-96 and James Hickey, "USCC Testimony on Central America," *Origins* 12, no. 41 (24 March 1983): 649,651-56.

[3]Canadian Conference of Catholic Bishops, "Ethical Choices and Political Challenges: Ethical Reflections on Canada's Socio-Economic Order," (Ottawa: Concanan, 1984). On pages five and six of this document are three principles found especially offensive to business leaders: 1) The basic rights of working people take priority over the maximization of profits and the accumulation of machines in an economic order; 2) In a given economic order, the needs of the poor take priority over the wants of the rich; 3) A socio-economic order which includes the participation of the poor takes precedence over an order which excludes them.

[4]Raymond Williams, *The Long Revolution* (London: Chatto and Windus, 1961), p. 106. The entirely of Chapter Four, "Images of Society," pp. 101-121, deserves study.

[5]Nathaniel Hawthorne, "Chiefly about War Matters by a Peaceable Man," in *Miscellanies: Biographical and Other Sketches and Letters,* vol 17 of Hawthorne's Works (Boston: Houghton Mifflin, 1900), pp. 405-406.

[6]An important, almost eccentric, modern witness against the symbolism of the military uniform from a gospel standpoint is that of Franz Jaegerstatter, who was executed for refusing even to don the German uniform during World War II. See Gordon Zahn, In Solitary Witness (Collegeville, Minn.: Liturgical Press, 1964).

Chapter 10
Youth and Social Justice: A Possible Combination?

Late in 1981, a small group of educators and youth ministers in New York City began planning the Youth for Peace Project, a program of youth education on issues of social justice and nonviolent peacemaking. The aim of this project was to train youth between the ages of 16 and 23 to find their own voice on social issues and to learn effective forms of action on these issues. The program stressed helping young people gain understanding and engage in effective action. An underlying conviction was that the most effective communicators to youth of information about peace and social justice issues were young people themselves.

In 1982, the organizing team of the project contacted every Roman Catholic diocese in the United States, inviting them to sponsor a Youth for Peace pilot weekend in 1983. Because Youth for Peace had raised a modest sum to support their efforts, the invitation explained that the Youth for Peace team would come at their own expense to direct the weekend if the local diocese would provide the place and the materials needed. The response to this invitation was feeble: only forty dioceses out of about 180 responded at all or asked for further information. Finally, about twenty dioceses decided on Youth for Peace weekends in 1983; five more sponsored weekends in 1984. The above figures show Youth for Peace to be a modest effort to do education for peace and social justice and to set some new directions for Roman Catholic youth ministry.

A somewhat unexpected result of the project has been the many questions raised about peace and justice education among youth leaders. Are young people interested in peace and justice? Are they ready for these questions? Are they capable of running their own organizations? Will they become upset and disoriented by knowledge about their own country's history of militarism and its collusion in injustice abroad? Will they become disruptive as they try out forms of action? Will social activism be rooted in prayer? Should we not ground them in piety first before offering programs of action? Rather than attempt to deal with all these questions, this chapter responds to two specific written comments made by an educator who was instrumental in getting Youth for Peace started in her own Midwest diocese. Her questions express the concerns of many others who have asked about Youth for Peace. Readers will note that my response attempts to "get behind" or question images and metaphors, a matter I treated in some detail in Chapter 2.

The Readiness for Social-Awareness Question

"One cannot just dunk young people into the whole issue of social awareness and expect them to swim." This image of dunking is a provocative one. Dunking connotes something violent and unwilled, at the very least something sudden and accidental. One goes from the state of dryness to the state of wetness, from being warm and comfortable in the sun on the dock to being jolted by the cold water, a dunk. It is sudden and sodden. Could a dunk be fatal? Do some who get dunked drown in the process? It would seem so.

So to the question of dunking young people in this sense, I must say, "No, one cannot do such a thing wisely." Suppose the young who get dunked cannot swim. Suppose the experience totally defeats them, causes a lifelong fear of water, or even, the worst possible case, causes them to drown. So I agree that dunking can be irresponsible, disastrous, and even fatal. However, on some issues, such as the weapons race, hunger, planned scenarios of war, and so forth, any first dose, even a gentle first dose, may come as a shock, maybe like stepping dry-shod into a puddle of muddy water. Some educators maintain that with some issues, such as hunger, an "immersion experience" is useful, to bring home to young people the enormity of the problem or to move the problem from the head to the belly. Thus, a twenty-four hour lock-in fast, involving prayer, fellowship, information-sharing, questioning, and action-planning may be a very effective way of getting one's feet wet. At least, it may help some young people to get into the life-giving swim.

Could it be that the enormity of social issues defeats us as educators when we think about the need to bring young people to awareness and action on these matters? In the phrasing of the sentence, "dunk them into the whole issue of social awareness," I find in "dunking" this sense that social issues are just too overwhelming to be faced. However, if at the outset we had had to take on the "whole issue," probably few of us would have been willing to undertake any kind of education, in science or literature, for example. In any case, there is no "whole issue of social awareness." Social awareness is an ability to recognize particular social issues about which one learns a bit at a time. Eventually, at some point, a person does realize that the public and social spheres deserve attention. Even then, however, the attention must be given gradually and cumulatively to specific issues, not to the whole socio-political area at once.

So if we wish to work toward social awareness, we must start with some concrete example of how a social system can defeat the ability of people to see each other as individuals and to care for each other. We can start with any particular issue that can be set forth specifically to engage the imaginations of young people. At is now obvious to readers of this book, my conviction is that peace is one such issue, and the horrors of war, though frightening to examine, can help particularize the importance of working for peace.

A further point about the issue of peace. Many young people in our time have a deep sense that something is very wrong in the world. They know that mutual attacks with nuclear weapons by just two nations could mean that all life on earth, not just human life, would be extinguished. This is a potential key to opening them to social reality. This may be the place from which to begin the slow walk toward social awareness. Even so, we can expect that dealing with peace or any other social issue will not be easy going for young people, because such issues produce anxiety and a sense of powerlessness.

The true problem is not one of leading them to "the whole issue of social awareness." The greater problem may actually be that some educational institutions refuse to address any of these matters. In a sense, the problem is a curriculum problem. Adults tend to teach what they consider to be important. They also tend to teach what they know and to steer carefully away from what they do not know. If those working with youth, including teachers, are themselves unattuned to social issues, then how can they help young people pay attention to them? One of the tyrannies of educational programs, and I do not locate them all in schools, can be the old curriculum, which may be imposed year in and year out, quite simply because that is the curriculum the educators are familiar with—that is what they know.

A new curriculum will never be translated into educational practice unless educators pay attention to it, master the ideas behind it, and begin the laborious task of making it accessible to young people. In a situation where social issues are effectively ignored by those working with youth, will not the raising of these issues be a shock indeed, like the first blast from a cold shower? If youth ministry has been retailing a view of the gospel as a message of comfort for oneself and one's intimates, will young people not be shocked when someone suggests otherwise?

Youth and Justice: The Prayer Question

A common objection to Youth for Peace among youth leaders was that their current projects were aimed at helping young people love themselves and understand that God loves them. Only after young people understand that Jesus is good news can they face these questions of justice. This objection, the "readiness objection," was actually the most common one that our Youth for Peace team faced. Our views on this question were based on the already-cited statement of the 1971 Synod of Bishops, "Justice in the World." According to that important document, attention to justice is a constitutive part of the preaching of the gospel. Notice how this principle rebuts the position of some leaders in youth ministry. They say social justice is consecutive, that is, it follows on loving oneself and loving God. The bishops' position, however, is that it is constitutive, that is, there is no true announcement of the gospel unless this element is present. The principle set forth by the bishops implies that even in work with very young children social justice is a constitutive element of good news.

In working with the Youth for Peace Project, we saw that some young people were more ready for the issues we raised than were some adult leaders. We had seriously misjudged the degree to which youth ministry leaders had formed their own consciences on the matters we were dealing with. Some of these older persons were as much at the beginning of paying disciplined attention to social justice as were the youth. It took courage for these leaders to acknowledge their own lack of information and understanding and to be willing to grow and learn with the young people one step at a time.

After several months of meeting and talking to diocesan youth leaders, I came to the realization that when leader after leader announced to us "Our kids aren't ready for this; maybe a few years down the road . . ." what they meant was that they themselves were not ready. It would have helped if some of those people could have—as some did years later—admitted, "Look, I know some young people need this opportunity, but I myself am not prepared to look 'the whole issue of social justice' in the eye. I have not been doing my homework on these questions. I have been overworked or asleep or just on the wrong questions. I need more time." Such an admission would have put the problem in its proper place.

The Progression Question

"It seems to me there is a progression—steps—that young people must generally go through, and as I see it, the top of the ladder is a willingness to become involved in the social issues of nonviolence and the gospel life." "Steps" is an important idea because it raises the question of whether an awareness of social justice issues is sequential, like a child's physical development, or as Kohlberg claims the stages of moral reasoning are. Or is this awareness, in some cases at least, achieved through a transformative leap, such as those Bernard Lonergan describes as intellectual conversion, moral conversion, and religious conversion? I am asking whether the sequential, step metaphor is the appropriate one here and whether a conversion metaphor is better. The step metaphor suggests that you cannot get to C until you go through A and B. The stress in such a metaphor is on sequence, almost like the sequence of steps a machine needs to manufacture a product. But the conversion metaphor is a transformative metaphor, suggesting that some progressions are made in leaps like the audacious ones made by the poet who suddenly sees the connections between matters previously perceived as unconnected. This is the sort of leap the scriptures describe as metanoia, a change of heart. Could the transformative metaphor be more appropriate for social justice education, or at least could it be a needed correlative to be sequential metaphor?

The problem of "how it happens" may be compounded by "the Siloe factor," which suggests that one can sit fruitlessly for thirty-eight years by the waters of transformation, because there was no one to help one into the waters. I was ready, but there was no one there to help. A punster might call this a sort of reverse dunk: you need the water, possibly ache for it, but remain distressingly dry because nobody gave the help you needed. Of course, there always will be some who have access to transformation but do not take advantage of it. Why did Teresa of Avila not go through the steps to holiness in her novitiate? Why did Charles de Foucauld live riotously for years before suddenly stepping out onto the long road that led eventually to Tamanrasset. Steps there may be, but wisdom about them lies in never forgetting that human development is rooted in mystery.

We in Youth for Peace have always held that nobody should attend our weekend of training who was not at least willing to examine questions of peacemaking and the possibility of nonviolence. We wanted at the very least a desire in our young people to take a look at these questions. We judged that such a desire was necessary for the educational phase of Youth for Peace. In a few cases young people opted to return home once they realized they had come to the weekend little aware of what the topic was. At least one young man confessed at the very end of the weekend that he had come because he knew he could not graduate from his Catholic high school unless he made a retreat and hoped ours might be the least religious of the weekends available. He then owned up to having undergone a transformation of sorts, which had yet to hold up before the great test of transformations: time. My point remains, however, that the educational phase of Youth for Peace required some desire and openness.

The commitment phase, on the other hand, is outside our control.

We took special pains to make clear to the participants on a weekend that the commitment to peacemaking and social justice is something each person must think about deeply. Youth for Peace weekends deliberately avoided all strategies towards enthusiasm and the ecstatic so common in youth weekends. If anything, we warned participants not to jump too gladly onto any bandwagon but to think the whole matter over carefully. The period between the actual Youth for Peace weekend and the follow-up weekends is for seeing if one is ready to begin a commitment to peacemaking and justice.

From the time I began to work with young people on social issues, starting around 1963 or 1964, I noticed there was a considerable time gap between my first presentation on any social matter and their acceptance of the information.[1] The gap was more pronounced if their own subculture had proposed to them a different view. Accepting a message about the evils of racism was not easy for young people from the East New York section of Brooklyn in those days. On the question of war and peace, some of those in 1966 who were most strongly in favor of the war in Vietnam later risked everything as conscientious objectors. The time gap was in some cases weeks and in others months. And some would return two years later to explain how slowly they had come to see the problems with their own eyes rather than through mine. What was exciting to me during our Youth for Peace weekends was that more young people than I expected seemed ready for commitment.

There do seem to be steps to commitment, though not in the Kohlbergian sense. An obvious and common sense sequence may be the progression from unfocused inattention, to focused attention on an issue, to action. Once commitment takes place, we can then only afterwards look back on the steps by which it developed. I have found helpful two different sets of such steps, one given by Michael Crosby and another by Maria Harris. It seems to me that these steps are not useful when programmed forward but rather help one look back, to see how one came to be in a new place.

Maria Harris described to me one day what she calls "moments" in education. She was deliberately seeking to use language that would avoid the sense of mechanistic sequence so popular in educational and social science literature. The first moment in Harris' sequence is silence, unawareness, and even a certain peacefulness that sometimes accompanies not being aware. One lacks the resources to break this silence of unawareness, and the silence is not being disrupted from outside. The second moment is awareness. One now knows and understands. A revolution has taken place in one's consciousness. What was previously not noticed is now front and center in awareness, and there is no way back to the previous state of not knowing. A certain naivete has been permanently disrupted. The third moment is that of mourning. We have now become aware of what we had previously not even considered. The world is more complex than we had realized. We have, for example, become aware of social structures, how they work, and whom they profit—and now we must let go of our previous innocence, our past misunderstandings, but also of our past allegiances. We have to mourn the loss of these inappropriate allegiances and of our former view of reality.

The fourth step is anger. My world has been upset. Why could I not have been left alone? What a fool I have been to have followed these previous misunderstandings or such and such a false way of life! Why did I not do something about these matters years ago? How could I have been so asleep? Such anger is partly directed against oneself, but also partly against those who colluded in our ignorance and partly against the old misunderstandings themselves.

The fifth moment is mutuality, a consequence of realizing that one cannot cope with the new awareness and more especially cannot take action on it without moving out to others who can work with us for change. A synonym for mutuality might be solidarity, a reaching out one's hands to others with whom one can take common action.

Michael Crosby, in his *Spirituality of the Beatitudes*,[2] outlines a series of shifts that disrupt a world view and create a new way of seeing. His shifts seem to expand on what happens between Harris' first moment of silence and the second one of awareness. The first shift according to Crosby is an experience that shakes our world view. I suspect that for some young people such a shattering experience occurs when they begin to understand the enormity of the danger of massive armaments. Following the shattering experience is a process of questioning our world view, including our faith. This questioning in turn eventually leads to a reconstruction of our world view and of our faith, which is followed by further exploration of the implications of our new understanding.

These descriptions of moments and shifts have been helpful to me in understanding the slow progress in young people from a naive world view to a better informed understanding of the world they live in. Understanding the moments of mourning, anger, and mutuality has helped me be more patient with the gradualness of progress and with the sometimes intense struggles some young people go through when they first face up to social justice matters. Those working on these matters with youth need to keep reflecting on their experience, as a way of reaching a more sophisticated understanding of what happens. Many young people do not move naturally toward mutuality. They need to be encouraged toward it, especially toward working with others in solidarity. Without mutuality or solidarity there is no true empowerment. Instead, young people tend to be defeated by the enormity of the issues facing them. However, when presented with concrete examples of effective common action and with specific lines of action they themselves can take, mutuality becomes more attractive and its resulting empowerment more of a possibility.

A final word about shifts and transformations. Recently I heard a youth leader suggest that for many people the shift toward concern for justice comes from meeting a victim. The point was made almost in passing, but it contains an important insight. I recognize that my own life was decisively changed when at age fourteen I first heard a graphic description of the machine-gunning of Jews in death pits in a forest in Germany. The soldier who did the gunning smoked a cigarette between groups of victims, who included many small children. The new groups, mostly family groups, stepped onto the bodies of the previous victims as they waited naked to die. With the vivid imagination of a fourteen-year-old, I "met" those victims and in their victimization realized for the first time the full potential of human evil. In Youth for Peace young people meet the victims of Hiroshima, and the victims of racism and also come to see the potential victimization of all they know in a nuclear holocaust. Such "meetings" should be an integral part of our gospel-based work with youth.

Resources for Peace and Global Awareness Ministry with Youth

Almost all denominations have excellent materials for use with the young. If peace and justice ministry is not being done among youth, it is not for lack of resources. Some of the materials are underused.

Here I list some additional resources on peace and global awareness readers might want to know about, examine, and use in their youth ministry.

1. Church World Service Office on Global Education, *Make a World of Difference: Creative Activities for Global Learning* (Baltimore: Office of Global Education, National Council of Churches, 1989). [A valuable handbook of perspectives and activities.]

2. Gerald Horne, ed., *Thinking and Rethinking U.S. History* (New York: Council on Interracial Books for Children, 1988). [A handbook designed to help teachers recover the lost voices of our history and some forgotten issues.]

3. The *Educating for Peace* materials developed by the joint effort of the Melbourne Catholic Education Office and the New

South Wales Department of Education. The various titles include:

A. Educating for Peace: Explorations and Proposals [A Report to the Curriculum Development Council] (Canberra: Canberra Publishing, 1987).

B. T.M. Doyle, ed., Educating for Peace: A Handbook for School Communities (Melbourne: Catholic Education Office, 1988).

C. T.M. Doyle, ed., Educating for Peace: P-6, A Teacher Handbook (Melbourne: Catholic Education Office, 1988).

D. T.M. Doyle, ed., Educating for Peace: 7-12, A Teacher Handbook (Melbourne: Catholic Education Office, 1988).

I consider these materials to be of high quality with special value for persons working in schools.

4. Important Resources Adaptable to Youth: Anne Hope and Sally Timmel, *Training for Transformation: a Handbook for Community Workers* Books I, II, III (Gweru, Zimbabwe: Mambo Press, 1984).

These books apply Paulo Freire's ideas on social transformation to particular situations; also available from The Grail, Loveland, Ohio.

5. Other Resources

Thomas Bright and John Roberto, *Justice* [Access Guides to Youth Ministry] (New Rochelle, NY: Don Bosco Multimedia, 1991).

Thomas Bright, ed., *Poverty: Do It Justice!* (New Rochelle, NY: Don Bosco Multimedia, 1993).

Thomas Bright and John Roberto, eds., *Human Rights: Do It Justice!* (New Rochelle, NY: Don Bosco Multimedia, 1993).

Barbara Lewis, *The Kid's Guide to Social Action* (Minneapolis: Free Spirit Publishing, 1991).

James McGinnis, ed., *Helping Teen Care* (New York: Crossroad, 1991).

These materials are relevant, up-to-date, and practical.

---

¹For years I had noted this time lag and assumed it simply took time for young people to accept different perspectives. Then, I came across Robert Selman's work on social perspective-taking and saw his clinical verification of my own experience of this matter of time lag. See Robert L. Selman, "Developmental Approach to Interpersonal and Moral Awareness in Young Children: Some Educational Implications of

Levels of Social Perspective-taking," in *Values and Moral Development,* ed. Thomas Hennessy (New York: Paulist, 1976), pp. 142-72, esp. pp. 165-66.

[2]Michael Crosby, *Spirituality of the Beatitudes: Matthew's Challenge for First World Christians* (Maryknoll, NY: Orbis, 1984).

Chapter 11
Youth Weekends: Assessing the Recent Past

Persons examining the development of youth ministry in the United States in the final four decades of the twentieth century will recognize the remarkable contribution made by the renewal of youth retreats. What the youth retreat renewal actually changed was a pattern of youth retreats that had been in place for eons, based on the tradition of silent monastic retreats in long use by active religious congregations. In these events youth participated mainly as listeners and worshippers, with some opportunities offered for individual counsel. Here focus was on the self, looking within to examine one's individual relationship with God. Stress tended to be on personal sin and individual transformation, with special concern for will power in the struggle for virtue. Out of the theological ferment immediately preceding Vatican II emerged such varied weekend models as Teens Encounter Christ (TEC), Search, Antioch, The Christian Awakening, and Christians on Retreat (COR). Here I wish to examine and assess these weekends of Christian living. A good place to begin such an assessment is with a brief history of the origins of some of these programs. Unfortunately, this history is relatively unknown.

A Historical Sketch

In 1961, the first English-Language Cursillo was held in the United States, having been brought from Spain four years earlier by United States Air Force cadets who had been stationed in Spain. There the Cursillo had been started by Bishop Juan Hervas as part of an experiment with ways of bringing the gospel to men, who in his culture tended to think of religion as a matter more appropriate to women.[1] He called his program the Cursillo de Christianidad, The "Little Course In Christianity." It was a "little course" because it was given for a short weekend and tried to deal with the heart of the gospel. His Cursillo stressed uncomplicated explanations of Christian faith with clear examples from everyday life. A good part of the weekend also involved ordinary Christians giving personal accounts of their own struggle to live the gospel. These were witness talks, living testimony from everyday folks.

They were given in a context of community of a group of persons joined by their common faith in the enduring presence of Jesus' spirit. Their common unity was celebrated in intense moments of prayer and worship, especially in the Eucharist.

The Cursillo spread through the spiritually dry landscape of Spain like wildfire. In the United States it spread even faster. Within two years after the English-Language Cursillo started, it had spread to twenty-three states.[2] When the full influence of the Cursillo over these years has been evaluated, we will find it had an astonishing influence on tens of thousands of adults, both Protestant and Catholic. The Cursillo enabled many of them to transform their knowledge of Jesus into the deep interiorized personal form of knowledge we call "faith knowing." Some of these adults saw the possibilities of the Cursillo for youth.

Two priests in the diocese of Brooklyn, Fathers Jim Tugwood and Doug Brown, made a Cursillo in late 1963 and immediately sought to adapt the basic format for young people. They recruited a youth team, trained them as facilitators, and in July 1964, in the basement of a high school, ran their first weekend, called simply "The Encounter," meaning an encounter with Jesus whom we call Christ. Clearly based on the Cursillo's theme of letting one's light shine, their program was later called "The Christian Awakening" in the early 1970s, when the word encounter came to connote nude group marathons. Their program has spread throughout the United States, and to Belgium and France. It has had a singular influence on Catholic youth work in Australia, New Zealand, and other South Pacific countries.[3]

More than a year before the Brooklyn program started, Father Peter Armstrong, director of the San Fransisco Catholic Youth Organization (CYO) program, launched the "Search for Christian Maturity," usually called the Search program. Although the Cursillo was already spreading on the West Coast in March 1963, the date of the first Search program, Armstrong's efforts developed from his experience with group dynamics and totally apart from any Cursillo influence. The initiative for Search came from young people, who asked for a weekend design within which they could function as team members. Experience- and community-centered rather than content-centered, Search has been devoted to the needs of youth as they defined them and has continued to adapt to the changing needs of youth in different areas. From the start Search avoided asking youth for the sort of total commitment to Jesus that might be appropriate for an adult at the end of a Cursillo. These unique aspects of Search, however, do not negate important similarities with the other youth weekend models.[4]

Because it could be tied to a well-organized existing network of diocesan CYO offices, Search grew fastest of the three emerging youth retreat models. Shortly after its start, dozens of diocesan CYO offices were running Search weekends. The biannual CYO convention became a special forum for spreading the excitement of Search, which featured a youth-centered rather than an adult-centered team.

Another well-known program is Teens Encounter Christ, which began in October of 1965 in the diocese of Lansing, Michigan. The program had been developed earlier that year as a project at the Loyola Pastoral Institute in Chicago. Possibly because of this background, TEC seems to have begun with a much more elaborately worked-out theory of what it was trying to accomplish than did either Search or The Encounter. TEC has used a much greater proportion of adults on its teams and has also incorporated a strong death-resurrection liturgical theme based on the Easter vigil.[5] However, anyone who compares the TEC weekend outline with that of a Cursillo will find a dramatic parallel between the two, including the presentations and meditations and activities such as chapel visits and the Sunday night reunion. In recounting the story of TEC beginnings, its co-founder, Matthew Fedewa has often explained his debt to the Cursillo.[6]

The most significant aspects of these various team-led, celebrative weekend experiences of the gospel message are remarkably similar and stand in contrast with the main features of the earlier silent retreats. Instead of looking at the self, these new retreats looked at the group; rather than within, they look around, catching a sense of the Spirit of Jesus present in the shared insight of those gathered together. Focus was more on the living church here and now in this place.

Under their varied names, these movements showed the Church that young people are open to the gospel message when presented in the proper context and in language that speaks to them. These weekends confirmed that young people need a chance to struggle to put their faith into their own words. Create a context in which the message can be whispered to them and they will learn to shout it. Further, these programs have centered evangelization and catechesis solidly within their proper atmosphere of celebration. These programs have shown that catechesis lends itself well to intense occasions such as these weekends.

In the years these weekends have been in operation, what has happened to those who have participated in them? Tens of thousands, perhaps hundreds of thousands, of young people have come to a Pentecost-like insight into the meaning of Jesus' message. Years later, their lives remain transformed by that basic experience. Some are now themselves in ministry with youth or in various other ministries because of their conversion and later experience on Youth Teams. Some are ministering in their workplace and through their family life, in a conscious pursuit of being faithful disciples.

These various weekend programs represent extraordinary achievements that have benefited young people in many parts of the world.
Whatever these achievements, we cannot expect that all these programs
have completed their evolution. Neither should they be encouraged to
rest on their laurels as if what they have achieved so far is the last word.
There is much more to be done, and my purpose here is to prompt some
discussion of what the "more" might be.

The Work Yet To Be Done

So far as I know, there have been few serious efforts to update the
youth weekends of Christian living. Apart from some minor adjustments,
the basic weekend programs are the same as they were in those exciting
days of experimentation in the mid 1960s.[7] However the world is not the
same, neither the wider sociopolitical world nor the theological world. It
is instructive to contrast the endless and sophisticated revisions in
catechetical school materials for young people since Vatican II with the
relatively unchanged materials of youth weekends.[8] Because printed
catechetical materials for youth have finally taken up the 1968 call of the
Medellin Conference to pay more attention to social issues, we now have
some fine texts on social justice for youth in schools. However, the world
reflected in the content of TEC, Antioch, Search and Christian
Awakening is still the relatively asocial world of 1964. The youth retreat
renewal has itself not undergone renewal. Lacking re-evaluation, renewal
may indeed be impossible. Could these programs be assumed to be the
last word in youth catechesis, beyond critical assessment? Because I fear
our weekends can easily overlook key features of the world of our day, I
invite those directing these programs to consider the following questions.

What happens when youth ministry conveys a clear impression
that the matters of moment for youth are all personal and interpersonal
matters? What happens when our agenda with youth deals only with
such issues as becoming self-directed, developing a sense of one's own
individuality, developing a healthy and Christian sexual self-understanding, developing a capacity to respond to God in prayerful ways, and coming to an appreciation of the personhood of others in one's family, one's
friends, and in all those one meets in the course of a day?

To be sure, we all recognize how essential these matters are for living as a Christian in our time. However, they are not sufficient as a full
presentation of the gospel. To limit our work to these matters is to give
the impression that they encompass all that is needed to be a follower of
Jesus in our day. Not a full loaf, they are insufficient to nourish the spirits
of young people. A youth ministry program that deals predominantly
with the self is not a complete presentation of the Christian message.

Such programs inadvertently deny youth access to questions that must be faced by followers of the one we call Lord. The world-wide proliferation of weapons, fueled in part by our own country; an unjust global economic system, working against millions of the world's poor; an epidemic of violence among U.S. youth that has gotten worse precisely in the years of what I am here calling the youth retreat renewal—these matters directly affect our young and their future but are given little if any attention on our weekends.

Can any program of youth weekends deal with all these matters on a single weekend? Common sense says no. But to run a weekend program on Christian living and to ignore the wider world is a mistake with long-range effects. Doing so situates the gospel in an out-of-this-world context. Shutting out this wider world makes it difficult if not impossible to connect the gospel message with matters that should be the most pressing ones for Christians in our day. What can be done? I have three specific suggestions that have more to do with long-range approach than with any dramatic shift to completely new directions. My proposals are about backgrounding, about a more careful presentation of Jesus, and about "second-level" weekend designs. These suggestions respect the value of the sorts of weekends we now have, but they also ask that we adjust our efforts in subtle ways.

Using "Backgrounding" More Intentionally

My main proposal is that we retain the main themes of our weekends but deal with them in a different mode. What I have in mind would be akin to taking a melodic line from Mozart or Chopin and putting it to a different beat, say a syncopated beat. Think about this for a moment. Where does the power of the particular presentations made during these weekends come from? The special significance of any presentation comes from the way it is introduced, the examples used to ground the message, and the specific applications that extend its significance to the lives of youth. I call this process backgrounding, that is, setting up a horizon within which we view the gospel.

Backgrounding is not something I seek to impose on our weekends. It is already there in great force. We use certain examples; we tell certain stories. These examples and stories bring to the fore certain elements and downplay others. In doing so we encourage one another to seek out other similar examples. In other words, what we say after the words "like" and "as" gives implicit directions to participants about how to explain their own lives. When I wanted to change the focus in my university course on marriage to reflect better the social pressures affecting the way students thought about the opposite sex and relationships in general, I found the best way to do so was not directly but obliquely, through the examples I used to anchor my lectures and in the kind of thinking I myself modeled for students in the course of class discussion. I also introduced or "framed" my lecture material in a way that called attention to the social climate affecting their attitudes. My basic material, for the most part, remained unchanged; the context I created for that material shifted intentionally and systematically.

The significance of what I am calling backgrounding became clear to me when I was searching out handbooks to use with students needing help with their writing. I collected and studied several such books to find techniques that might be useful to those in my classes. All these books were filled with examples of various kinds of prose, illustrations of writing in single sentences, in paragraphs, and in full essay form. In only one book, however, did every example, every illustrative sentence, deal with some aspect of the social world. This book was *Thinking Straight*, by Monroe C. Beardsley, then a professor of English and aesthetics at Temple University.[9] When one finished Beardsley's course in clear writing, one had a strong sense that the social world is *the* world needing our attention—even though he never once mentioned this matter. It was like going into my favorite New York City delicatessen to buy bread but having in my nostrils the whole time the distinct aroma of various kinds of coffee on sale in the back of the store. Leaving that story you carry the bread and the memory of that marvelous aroma with you.

I propose we use backgrounding more intentionally in all our youth programs. This backgrounding needs to reflect more of the wider social world in which we live. Otherwise we give an impression that the gospel affects only one's private world, that it is a matter of personal choice only and ultimately a matter of personal decision and will. Gustavo Gutierrez suggests that such an approach does not go far enough: "In our relationship with God and with others there is an inescapable personal dimension: to reject a fellow human being, a possibility implicit in our freedom, is to reject God as well."[10] Notice how Gutierrez re-names the personal dimension of faith. Instead of using "personal" to mean the self, that is "we" or "I," he suggests that the proper understanding of the personal in faith also looks to the person of the other.

The gospel is a matter of choices, *but not only of choices*. The great evils of our day arise not from individual malevolence but from structures and systems that are evil and demeaning to persons. My hope is that our weekends will enable young people to begin to think about these systems, beginning first, with the fact that they exist and that they are a religious problem. The way we speak and deal with religious issues can in effect deny such systems exist or that they count for anything. Of course little can be done if those directing these weekends themselves work as if the world of interpersonal relationships were the only world.

Many, however, believe that concern for the social or systemic dimension of the gospel is something that should be dealt with on some later weekend, not on the occasion of the first evangelization which summons young people to conversion. They claim it is important to introduce the young to the person of Jesus, to let them encounter him, and then, after they are well-grounded in prayer and communion, to deal with matters of social justice. Such thinking, as I have already pointed out in these pages, claims that these aspects of the gospel are consecutive, that personal relationship with Jesus as Lord is to be followed by the call for justice. The bishops of the Roman Catholic Church, however, have taken a different position on this question. At their 1971 Synod in Rome, they clearly stated that "action on behalf of justice and participation in the transformation of the world fully appear to us as a constitutive dimension of the preaching of the gospel. . ."[11] Concern for justice is not a follow-up to effective evangelization; there is no effective evangelization unless this concern is part of it, at least in a backgrounding way.

This same synod had some important things to say about education, which might have a bearing on weekends of Christian living:

> The still predominant method of education today favors a narrowminded individualism. A great part of the people are actually swallowed up in a boundless overestimation of possessions. The school and the mass media stand now even under the power of the established "system" and so they can only form persons in the way they are needed by the "system"...not new persons, but only a reproduction of the traditional types.

The bishops then describe the proper way of education, according to the radical demands of the gospel.

> The right education demands a transformation of heart; fundamental to this is the admission of sin in its personal as well as its social forms. Education must emphasize a totally human way of life in justice, in love and simplicity. It must awaken the capacity of critical reflection on our society and on its current values; it must stimulate the readiness to reject these values when they no longer contribute to helping all persons come to their rights.[12]

So I am proposing that weekends of Christian living could do with a re-examination of their presentations and meditations, to see if they could be recast or adjusted to pay greater attention to important aspects of our current world. Perhaps now is the time for the renewal of the renewal. Such a re-examination does not have to be done hastily. It could involve many concerned persons working together over an extended period. Such a project could be a marvelous process of self-initiated learning for those who choose to undertake it.

A More Radical Presentation of Jesus

Another matter I wish to propose is a re-examination of the Jesus we are presenting. I have been concerned about the vision of Jesus presented in many different programs for middle-class youth. This Jesus tends to represent the dominant concerns of the moderately well-off and privileged.[13] The dominant concern of the middle-class tends to be greater comfort, and thus the middle-class Jesus is presented as the one who comforts. Overlooked is the Jesus who not only comforted but who also confronted and challenged. The middle-class Jesus is not the "man for others"; the middle-class Jesus is the man for us. Jon Sobrino points out that this is not a new problem.

> In [19th and early 20th century] liberal theology Jesus represents in its sublimest form the good that is to be found in human beings. He thus becomes, in his own historical context, the supreme embodiment of the virtues of the middle-class citizen of the late nineteenth century in whom life and culture, throne and altar, existence and virtue are all in harmony.[14]

Such a presentation of Jesus is basically self-centered, unable to move beyond God's love *for us*. As essential as it is to understand Jesus as God-*with-us* and as God's special gift *to us*, there is another side to discipleship, which focuses on God's love for The Other.

In the gospels Jesus calls us to embrace the poor and the weak and those who do not fit. Jesus continually calls attention to the social situations that needed to be changed and to the people who suffered in these social situations, the poor. Who are the poor, as presented in the gospels? One writer describes them as follows.

> Although the term "poor" in the gospels does not refer exclusively to those who were economically deprived, it does include them. The poor were in the very first place the beggars. They were the sick and disabled who had resorted to begging because they were unemployable and without a relative who could afford to or was willing to support them.
>
> There were of course no hospitals, welfare institutions or disability grants. They were expected to beg for their bread. Thus, the blind, the deaf and dumb, the lame, the cripples and the lepers were generally beggars.
>
> Then there were the widows and orphans: the woman and children who had no one to provide for them and, in that society, no way of earn-

ing a living. They would have been dependent upon the almsgiving of pious societies and the temple treasury. Among the economically poor one should also include the unskilled day-laborers who were often without work, the peasants who worked on the farms and perhaps the slaves.

On the whole, the suffering of the poor was not destitution and starvation except during a war or a famine. They were sometimes hungry and thirsty, but unlike millions today, they seldom starved. The principal suffering of the poor, then as now, was shame and disgrace. As the steward in the parable says, "I would be too ashamed to beg." (Lk 6:3)

The economically poor were totally dependent upon the "charity" of others. For the Oriental, even more so than for the Westerner, this is terribly humiliating. In the Middle East, prestige and honor are more important than food or life itself. Money, power, and learning give a person prestige and status because they make the person relatively independent and able to do things for other people. The really poor person who is dependent upon others and has no one dependent upon him/her is at the bottom of the social ladder. That person has no prestige and no honor. That person is hardly human. That person's life is meaningless. A Westerner today would experience this as a loss of human dignity.[15]

Whereas the gospels are filled with Jesus' passion for the poor and for justice for the poor, sometimes our own accounts of Jesus' life omit this central concern. We cannot understand the message of Jesus unless we understand the biblical idea of the kingdom of God, which was a call for justice.[16] As preached by Jesus, the kingdom of God assumed that something was wrong with a social order treating some people as things; it must be corrected. Change of heart is essential for righting wrong, but so are change of unfair public policy and change of systems that are evil. What made the preaching of Jesus so dangerous was his call for a new order that sided with the poor, replacing greed with sharing. When the powers-that-be realized this side of his preaching, they decided to get rid of him.

I propose that weekends of Christian living for youth need to reclaim this Jesus, the man who was eliminated because he exposed the greed of the rich. They need to reclaim the Jesus who called so strongly for nonviolence and love of enemies that some of his later followers resigned from military service as soon as they became Christians."
These weekends need to reclaim the Jesus who called for the transformation of social structures. To ignore this Jesus is to distort the paschal mystery. What is obviously involved here is another stage in the develop-

ment of weekends of Christian living, a stage that will pay greater attention to the world in which we live and will prepare youth for a lifetime of paying attention to issues of justice, a stage that will present a portrait of Jesus more faithful to the historical person who was "terminated" because of his challenges to unjust structures.

New Weekend Designs

Years ago the youth retreat movement discovered the genius of the dialogue format on weekends and handed over the discovery to youth leaders worldwide. However, in my judgment, the movement has not utilized the full possibilities of that discovery. Why have we not developed second-level weekends for young people wanting to go deeper into the mystery of Jesus? Could we not, for example, develop such weekends for members of our weekend leadership teams, to assist them coming to a deeper understanding of Jesus, including the complex period in which he lived, his teaching, and the communities that followed him? For the young people who leave our weekends eager to translate their experience into daily action, do we not need second-level weekends dealing specifically with social issues and with ways of helping their peers understand and deal with these social issues?

A common problem of all these weekend programs is the tendency of the participants to want to hold on to their original experience and then recapture it by coming back to other weekends. Someone has called those who are frantic about such repeat experiences "weekend junkies." These young people want to go back. We need to encourage them instead to go on, to go deeper, to take up more courageously the challenge of the gospel. That encouragement may take the form of further weekend experiences at a much deeper level.

Most weekend programs acknowledge that they are not the total answer. The above suggestions do not ask them now to seek to become "total" programs. Instead, they suggest the possibility of going a bit farther in their ministry with youth. None of these new directions needs to be decided overnight. Yet, with some planning, weekends can be designed around themes such as peacemaking and nonviolence;[17] the Jesus who was criminalized because of his call for social change; and around issues such as world hunger, weapons production, or the more just distribution of wealth. When young people from these weekends of Christian living become involved with even younger people in order to help them understand such issues, then we will have launched a new day in youth ministry, another stage of a renewal with a new range of achievements to celebrate in the name of Jesus.

[1]John McLaughlin, "I Made a Cursillo," *America* 110 (18 January 1964): 94-101.

[2]Ibid. The rapid growth of the Cursillo is hinted at in the sudden spate of periodical articles on the movement, beginning in early 1962.

[3]The information given here on the Christian Awakening is, as far as I know, not documented. It comes from my own knowledge of the events and from conversations with leaders in Australia and New Zealand.

[4]This information on Search was given me by Msgr. Peter Armstrong and Fr. Michael Harriman, Youth Director in San Francisco, in detailed telephone conversations. I am indebted to the kindness of both.

[5]See "Introduction and Explanation of the TEC Experience," published by the St. Louis TEC Center.

[6]James Brown, "TEC in Perspective," videotape, 27 July 1983, distributed by the Youth Ministry Office, Diocese of Green Bay, Wisconsin.

[7]It may be significant for leaders for youth weekends to know that Bishop Juan Hervas and other early Cursillo leaders were adamant that nothing should be changed in its format, "not a single iota." An extensive critique of that stance, as well as of the pre-Vatican II theology of the Cursillo appears in Antoninus Feeney, "A Critique of the Theology Underlying the Cursillo" (M.A. thesis, Catholic University of America, 1971).

[8]This same contrast is pointed out by Feeney in his "Critique": "Curiously enough children's textbooks published in the U.S. contain more new, rich theological material than do the doctrinal outlines of the Cursillo, even those recently revised" p. 5.

[9]Monroe Beardsley, *Thinking Straight: Principles of Reasoning for Readers and Writers* Fourth Edition (NJ: Prentice-Hall 1975).

[10]Gustavo Gutierrez, *We Drink from Our Own Wells* (New York: Orbis/Dove, 1984), p. 97.

[11]Synod of Bishops, 1971, *Justice in the World,* in David J. O'Brien and Thomas A Shannon, eds., *Renewing the Earth: Catholic Documents on Peace, Justice, and Liberation* (New York: Image Books, 1977), pp. 390-408.

[12]Ibid., pp. 401-402. The translation used here, however, is the one found in, Adolf Exeler, "The Social Dimension of the Fundamental Truths of the Faith," *East Asian Pastoral Review* 20, no. 2 (1983): 136. I recommend Exeler's article as an important one for reference in any revision project for youth retreats.

[13]See, Raymond Brown, *The Churches the Apostles Left Behind* (New York: Paulist, 1984) pp. 84-101. This book documents the various stresses or angles of Christian vision among the different communities of Jesus' followers. Varied

emphases are not to be deplored. What needs to be resisted is a class bias as a basic lens through which we view the gospel. For a case in point, notice Brown's the treatment of the Johannine Community's emphasis on an attachment to Jesus that was personal but not individualistic.

[14]Jon Sobrino, *The True Church and the Poor* (New York: Orbis, 1984), p. 25. For more on this important problem, see Robert Coles and George Abbott White, "The Religion of `The Privileged Ones'," Cross Currents 31, no. 1 (1981): 1-14. See also the distinction between prophetic concern and self-indulgence made by Donald Evans in Struggle and Fulfillment (New York: Collins, 1979), pp. 142-47. finally, see Dorothee Soelle, Suffering (Philadelphia: Fortress, 1975).

[15]Albert Nolan, *Jesus Before Christianity* (New York: Orbis, 1978), pp. 22-23.

[16]See Jon Sobrino, *Christology at the Crossroads* (New York: Orbis, 1978), pp. 41-78.

[17]A subtle study of the tradition of nonviolence in the early church is Knut Willem Ruyter, "Pacifism and Military Service in the Early Church," *Cross Currents* 32, no. 1 (1982): 54-70. The most complete recent treatment may be found in Jean-Michel Homus, *It is Not Lawful for Me to Fight: Early Christian Attitudes Toward War, Violence, and the State* (Scottsdale, Pa: Herald, 1980).

Chapter 12
Youth Weekends: A Critical Look Forward

The essays in this book show clearly my special interest in "youth weekend" movement. A fair portion of my writing about youth, including all writing about Youth for Peace, has this movement either in its foreground or background. In this reflection, I seek to raise some questions about the future of these weekends of Christian living, as I have liked to call them. I started my work on this essay by seeking to make proposals for the future of the movement but came to see that "proposals" was not the right category for what I wanted to say. Proposals are more finished, more thought through, than are questions. A question is often a proposal in the process of being born, a latent proposal. To use the analogy of a funnel, the question is the wide, hopper end; the proposal is the narrow funnelled end. Here then I want to raise three questions about youth in the coming church and how our weekends may help youth face this emerging church—and indeed, help the church face youth of the future. I will end with some suggestions for structural shifts in our actual weekend program.

In what I have to say I am making some assumptions about the functioning of these weekends in most denominations. First, I assume the youth weekend population is by far made up of middle and upper class young people. I also assume that in addition to the initial conversion-type weekends, there exist other kinds of weekends, longer-than-weekend events, and also non-weekend follow-up programs. Not all of what I want to say can be applied to the first-conversion weekends. Finally I also assume some youth leaders are already working on the questions I raise.

First Question: The Times We Are Living In

My first question is related to the times we are living in and where we are located in them. Is the world that provides the background of our retreats, the world the young are inheriting? Another way of asking this question might be: Are our weekends in fact dealing with our contemporary world? Some might object to this last way of putting it as silly. They might say, "Of course they deal with the contemporary world, because

our young people are in that world. They certainly aren't living in the
world of twenty years ago. The weekend programs can't *not* be in the
contemporary world; otherwise the young wouldn't attend."

However my question is getting at what kind of contemporaneity
our weekends have. I would say the deepest overall up-to-date-ness of
youth ministry in the U.S. is in the area of entertainment, especially
music. Listen to Don Kimball's "Music with a Message" tapes and you'll
see the intense *now* character of what he does. This sort of contemporaneity can be expanded, should be expanded, to include even the world
about to break in on us, the world-about-to-be. Acutely aware as they are
of emerging trends in music, entertainment and fashion, could many
young people be living in the world I am about to describe but quite
unaware of it?

Speaking in 1991 at a celebration of the 100th anniversary of
Rerum Novarum, an important Roman Catholic teaching on justice,
Walter Burghardt asked and answered a pressing question: "Have you
heard the latest figures on `the global village'? " His answer:

> If our world were a village of 1,000 people, that village would have the
> following residents: Asians 565; Europeans 219; Africans 86; South
> Americans 80; North Americans 60. Of these people, 60 would control
> half the income, 500 would be hungry; 600 would live in shantytowns,
> 700 would be illiterate.[1]

This is the world our young people are living in and are inheriting,
though they may not be aware of it.

Writing a few months earlier than Burghardt, Robert Reich, then a
Harvard political economist, noted that in 1991 the top one-fifth of U.S.
wage earners took home more money than the other four-fifths put
together.[2] Reich also noted that U.S. households with less than $10,000
gave an average of 5.5% of their earnings to charity of a religious organization, but those making more than $100,000 gave only 2.9%. After the
1988 tax code change, taxpayers earning over $500,000 slashed their
average charitable donations from $47,500 in 1980 to $16,000 in 1988
[i.e., by two-thirds].[3] Reich went on to point out there are now in the U.S.
more private security guards protecting the property of those who can
pay for their special protection than there are public police officers.

Recently I was pondering these economic facts as I drove on a
windy day along Route 195, the huge north-south coastal highway in the
Northeast, near Boston. Suddenly I saw off in the distance an immense
U.S. flag fluttering in a stiff breeze. It seemed so large that I first thought
it might have been half the size of a football field. I began to wonder what
site it marked. It couldn't be a municipal building, such as a city hall or a
fire station, as those buildings are usually regulated as to flag sizes.

Maybe it was a local political group that needed to wave a very big flag. Could it be an American Legion or Veterans of Foreign Wars Post? My curiosity was alert as I raced along to the place where the flag bristled quite close to the highway. The massive flag made a massive statement. Whose statement?

As I zipped past the spot I saw clearly that it was not a political party headquarters at all; it was a Cadillac dealership. In a flash it occurred to me how appropriate it was. The society that flag stands for is much kinder to the people who drive Cadillacs than it is, say, to people I regularly see with a kind of conveyance very different from a Cadillac: the homeless pushing their worldly belongings in shopping carts. If we applied the logic of size to the societal care given the homeless, they might sport on their shopping carts a flag much smaller than a postage stamp. Instead of this biggest imaginable flag, they would have the smallest imaginable one, if one at all.

The American Economic Association determines "the rich" as families with incomes more than nine times the poverty line. Some of my students and not a few adults I know would add, "Well, they earn it; they work harder to get what they get." In 1989 the average compensation for the chief executive of a big company was 93 times the average pay of a factory worker and 72 times that of a teacher.[4]

This statistical rendition may be boring or even offensive to some, and certainly at the very moment such statistics are cited, they are becoming out-of-date. What does any of this have to do with ministry with youth or with our weekends of Christian living? I say they have to do with the world in which we are living and which we must not neglect in our ministry to and with the young. But even without invoking a gospel perspective, I claim these figures represent the new social order our young people are moving into. In the mythicized year 2000, our current sixteen-year-olders will be at an age more deeply affected by these inequalities. Nearly half (44%) of the new jobs created from 1979 to 1985 paid less than the poverty-level income, while just about 10% of new jobs were in the high-wage category (above $29,600). Commentators note that "the increase in poorly paid jobs is not restricted to minorities and women. Since 1979, nearly three-quarters of the net job gains of white men have been at the low end of the [wage] spectrum—more than for any other demographic group."[5]

Considering these economic pressures, will the young now in our retreat programs undergo in the years of the twenty-first century marital and family struggles as they move through early adulthood and into marriage? Will they need two incomes to finance housing and children? Will those among them wishing to stay home and nurture young children be able to do so? Will economic pressures put emotional strains, possibly fatal ones, on parenting and marriage? All who care about the young may want to ponder these questions. Though the facts and figures cited here quickly go out of date, the financial strains of early adulthood are not far down the road for a sixteen year old and are being caused by policy decisions at the moment one reads these words.

For example, will these young people reaching their mid-twenties after the year 2000 want to buy homes? In the Reagan years the federal housing budget was slashed by 80%, but of course some people continued to receive subsidies, many of them direct, like tax deductions for mortgage interest payments, a form of social welfare that is not called welfare. Counting both direct and hidden subsidies, the housing situation at the end of the 80's was as follows:

—the 25% of U.S. households with annual incomes under
   $10,000 received 13% of all federal housing subsidies;
—the 27% of households with incomes between $10,000 and
   $20,000 received 7% of all federal subsidies;
—the 21% of households with incomes between $20,000 and
   $30,000 received 13% of all federal subsidies;
—the 20% of households with incomes between $30,000 and
   50,000 received 44% of all subsidies; and
—the 7% of all households with incomes over $50,000 received
   24% of subsidies.[6]

These inequities will affect our young people. The problem with such figures themselves is that they overly stress life in the U.S., whereas our national share of the global pie is so far beyond our proportion of the world's population that it staggers the mind. Another problem with this information as I have presented it here is that I have not yet mentioned a gospel perspective or response. As followers of Jesus, this information creates for us a crisis of conscience about what we are paying attention to and about our patterns of living our daily lives. Unfortunately, there are ways of talking about God that give a clear impression that these situations do not exist or that they do not matter. *Will we stop talking about God in ways that hide the significance of justice for our understanding of God's message to us?*
Seminarians in a recent course I taught found great scandal, not in the global or national inequities cited above, but in the claim that there should be a "preferential option for the poor." The scandal for them was not that governmental policies clearly side with the wealthy but in implying that God took sides and contested the priorities of the rich. I can only presume that their whole lives religious leaders have been talking to them about God in ways that ignored God's word about justice. How will

we find ways of speaking about God that establish God's scripture-based passion for eliminating the conditions of misery? One way of course is to study how Jesus himself spoke of this matter.

To run a weekend for young people in a way that encourages them to overlook this situation in which they live is to foster in them religious insensitivity and to be ourselves unfaithful to Jesus' teaching. On the other hand, as I have already indicated in this book, I have always believed there are inappropriate ways of raising these matters with the young. One of them is to imply they should go out and change the world singlehandedly or that somehow these conditions exist because of their individual selfishness. However, *any* calling of their attention to serious but ignored issues will tend to shock and upset them. They are not responsible for the world's evil in the sense that they caused it. They are response-able in the sense of being able to pay attention to this world and to ponder what part their own lives might have in dealing with that world.

Second Question: The Church We Are In

My second question is about the church we are in. Will we so deal with our young people that we are preparing them for the coming church? Most of us are aware that youth are not just the future of the church; they are also the present of the church. Further, they are the presence among us of a future church. Could we be preparing them for a church that is fading away? Will the young women on our weekends who possess acute feminist sensitivities find themselves eventually, as are so many religious feminists, in an ecclesial landscape that is alien and alienating?

One of the standout features of youth weekends over the past thirty years or so has been their ability to invite the alienated young into fellowship in the Spirit of Jesus. I was amazed in 1964 at the ability of a weekend of Christian living to disclose to the very alienated that Jesus had whispered to human beings a liberating secret about the meaning of life, a secret these alienated ones had been longing for. And yet, even then at the start of Vatican II, an urgent problem for these new retreat programs was the distance between the ecclesia the youth had lived on the weekend and the one they went back to for Sunday Eucharist. In those days the basic difference was the kind of participation available to the young. On the weekend, they had a say, lots of say, the chance to speak their minds and hearts, to cry if they wanted, to rant and rave if they chose—and to be heard. And the word of God came tumbling off human tongues, sometimes in halting or choked phrases—filled with power in the very effort to get them out. In a society that treats the young as consumers—of manufactured products, of spectator sports and entertainment, of education, and of religious meaning, our retreats had given them a chance to become *original co-producers of religious insight.* What an exhilaration for them to find they had this power within. And then—at least this is how so many told it to me—they went back to the zone of no-say, to the place where they were to be mute, where they could only listen, despite the ritual amens and thanks-be-to-Gods. They were back to being consumers of the religious insights of others, almost always those of older males.[7] In my view this situation has changed little in thirty years.

Speaking to a national planning group, theologian Ladislaus Orsy claimed that a characteristic of the modern church is a "strong and pervasive sense of participation," meaning, a strong and pervasive desire for participation and a sense that one should have a right to so participate. He then went on to describe the problem as a systemic one.[8] The following is my own version of what he said.

1. Laity wish to participate more deeply in the decisions made by clergy about matters in the church that affect them, but are frustrated because they are not given the opportunity.
2. Clergy wish to participate more intensely in the decisions made by bishops about matters of diocesan policy that affect them, but are frustrated because they are not given the opportunity.
3. Church leaders wish to participate by having a larger share in issues affecting their wider geographical region and their country—for instance, the appointment of new bishops, but they are frustrated because they are not allowed to.
4. Women who participate a lot at a very specific level as catechists and providers of services men don't wish to perform wish to speak out more on issues affecting the church. They also wish to have access to the priestly roles now only open to men, but they are frustrated because they are not given the opportunity, but based on a special set of reasons, those of gender.
5. I could say that young people are so long in this systematic diminishment of gifts that they figure there is no use in even trying to have a say, and so they just drop out; but that is not exactly the case. Ironically, in some parish youth ministries, young people have more say in church decisions affecting them than do many adults.

What can be done in this situation? Here I can only sketch a proposal that would at the very least need a weekend like this one to deal

with it in depth. Most of my ideas come from an article by Catholic
University theologian, David Power, entitled, "Households of Faith in the
Coming Church."[9] Power point out that the church has always had many
small, informal and spontaneous groups, associations and communities.
The ones he gives special attention are those outside the formal structures, formed partly because of disenchantment with the canonically rec-
ognized ecclesial organization. Most Protestant denominations were originally formed out of just such disenchantment. Such groups arose from a
creative, gospel-centered critique of the established church order, a critique they backed up by alternative ways of living.

Power probes history to find examples marked by a God-centered
freedom as a gift of the Spirit. Such a freedom gave rise to the remarkable spiritual energy that found outlets in the works of mercy and also in
emphasis on choice and decision. Contesting a church that had sacral-
ized its own structures and becoming thereby blind to anti-gospel elements in its own organization, these communities of disenchantment
developed highly participatory structures. Power's conviction is that

> it is true of every renewal movement in the history of the church that, in
> a way peculiar to its own time and in face of the second temptation, to
> wit, an accommodation with the prevalent temporal power, it has had at
> its core a renewed awareness of the...[importance] of evangelical pover-
> ty. (p. 240)

Power finds such groups are an increasing phenomenon in today's
church.

Just as Francis broke with the emerging money economy of his
time, and through the vow of poverty, with the church "benefices" and
the collection of church tithes in his time, so today many of the emerging
households of faith struggle with questions of gospel poverty, concern
for the poor, and "a search for the living meaning of poverty in Christ."[10]
These groups exist not only in Latin America but in neighborhoods familiar to many of us—though the fact of these groups may not be familiar to
us. I encourage readers to examine Power's essay for themselves. In his
own words, here is a summary of the main features of the households of
faith most deeply faithful to the gospel.

a) the form of life will be that of evangelical poverty;
b) the key to their relation to society will be emancipatory praxis,
   the desire and the struggle to come to the release of those
   who suffer bondage in the midst of progress, a resistance to
   the many forms of violence whereby the poor are oppressed;
c) their liturgies will be forceful commemorations of the suffering
   and resurrection of Jesus Christ, into which will be gathered a

memory of all suffering and of all the forgotten and unnamed of past and present;

d) because their members possess a strong sense of the freedom that comes with the gift of the Spirit, they will develop community structures that are participatory and respectful of a variety and multiplicity of gifts. (p. 244.)

Although all these features are important, here I want to highlight the participatory forms of these households would have for young people. Youth remain the presence among us of a coming church, and I suspect some of them will not survive in many parishes as currently structured.

These households could, and I believe would, offer young people a chance to become equal partners in a quest for discipleship. What I am thinking of are inter-generational groups that include youth, instead of peer groups of youth, though if peer groups were the only option, they would be better than nothing. Such groups would be zones where the young and others could talk out as co-searchers the problem Jesus' message confronts us with in this culture. A spirituality of poverty in a time of socially legitimated greed will be a spirituality of struggle for any of us, and very much so for young people who may not have yet considered the significance of Jesus' teaching on the relation of discipleship and poverty.

So what I am proposing is establishing house church groups as an option for those on our weekends looking for some way of living out with others the baptismal gospel call they may have finally "heard" on a weekend. Such groups would have to be seen as much more than another of the elusive "follow-up" programs retreat leaders have been searching for, like a holy grail, since the beginning of the youth retreat renewal. My questions are: Will we try? Which of us ourselves are ready for this step?

Third Question: The Problem of Life Structure

My third question has to do with the stage of life young people themselves are in: the young adult transition. Will we help them become aware of the importance for discipleship of the patterns of living they are in the midst of establishing? They are in a period of life in which they are forging a life structure decisive in many ways for the rest of their years.

A priest I know who teaches in an all-boys Catholic high school in New York City told me a few years ago that many of the boys he teaches have worked out for themselves a kind of no-fault Christianity. From a religious standpoint, how they behave does not matter. What is essential is to have good intentions, especially about God. God will love them no matter what they do. Specific ways of living, concrete deeds, do not come into the picture. This attitude directly contradicts the intense focus on behavior in the early church's practice of the catechumenate. This was a period of initiation, of testing, to see if the persons seeking baptism could actually walk the walk of discipleship. But of course our own scriptures are clear about the priority of deeds over words; they even have a way of talking about "Word" that ties word intimately to action, to realization of word.

One of the reasons parents are so concerned about their children is that the child is forming his or her ways. Infants are basically without habits; they are being formed almost the way the child's bones are being formed. If a child does not wear properly fitting shoes, his or her feet may not grow properly or be formed properly. Sometimes a child's whole hip and leg must be put into a cast for months to ensure proper bone formation. On all these matters parents are aware of the importance of helping the child learn proper habits of eating, of personal hygiene and cleanliness, of carefulness and neatness. Habits are bound to be formed. There is no doubt about that. But if it is necessary that habits be formed, it is not necessary that these be good habits. Good habits sometimes need to be developed through great painstaking care on the part of parents.

This same process of forming habits or *ways* keeps on developing as one gets older. Eventually we all have our own personal habits, our own ways, in the handling of so many very tiny matters, of doing dishes and of cleaning up, of getting dressed, of going to bed, of taking a shower, and so on. The closer one gets to an older person, the more one becomes aware of these ingrained habits and of how they need to be respected at least in general. Should any of these habits prove undesirable for any of many possible reasons, they cannot be easily turned around, any more than one can easily convince a child that s/he should not take some toy to bed at night—once the child has gotten into the habit of doing so.

What many young people do not realize—and what few who work with them reflect on enough—is that in one's late teens one is in a key phase of establishing one's *ways*. During those years, one is developing a structure of living that will direct one's life for a long time to come: tastes in food; patterns in the use of time; preferences and even styles of watching TV; ways of being with older people—or of not being with them; ways of behaving in groups; ways of studying, of reading, even of reading the newspaper—or a way of not reading it. Being formed are ways of driving a car, ways of using alcohol, ways of relating to the opposite sex, ways of dealing with the truth, ways of getting one's own will, and far from the least important, ways of thinking about and using money. Behind the nexus of these patterns is a life structure that affects commitments.

A life structure is a pattern of choices and ways of living out choices that become the established way for a person. These patterns are belief systems written into one's behavior. Once established the pattern tends to perdure, even in spite of shifts in location, career, or even marriage partner. When young people say they want to live one reality, let's say, a religious reality, but actually live another, the reason is that they have structured this other reality into their behavior. As a college teacher I have over and over again met very good people with very good intentions who are stuck in the wrong life structure, say together with a particular group of friends. Our friends, their attitudes and behavior, tend to structure our own attitudes and behavior. What has interested me in conversations with 18-22 year olds is that some—more than I would ever have thought—harbor an inner sense, a lingering suspicion, they may have ended up with the wrong friends. Publicly they will defend their friends and reject the suggestion that it could be appropriate to re-consider one's choice of friends; but privately some struggle with this question. The patterns of behavior initiated among a group of friends are patterns they are stuck in but at the same time may no longer be appropriate to the persons they are coming to be.

For one small but important example, we now know that groups of young men can develop ways of talking about women and ways of handing on to each other myths about what women want in a heterosexual relationship that can lead to a much higher incidence of rape among those groups, say, members of athletic teams or fraternities. In other words, some patterns of speech about women are concrete verbal ways of demeaning women. This speech behavior is a true behavior that prepares for the physically abusive—and violent—behavior of rape itself. I tell the men students in my marriage course that the first step in changing the way one thinks about women is to change the way one talks about women—including one's acceptance of demeaning comments about women by others, including friends. Patterns of speech are part of the structure of our behavior.

A Bucknell University social psychologist studying group sexual assaults on college campuses wrote the *The New York Times*[11] and pointed out that group sexual assaults on or near campus usually occur in all male housing with other men as onlookers. He noted that such groups of men develop their own group norms with regard to women. *They regard men accused of rape as victims and women as victimizers,* even when the men admit to some form of reprehensible group exploitation. He went on to say: "If those men who confess to such exploitation while denying criminal culpability are anyone's victims, they are victims of their own group norms. Such groups of men on campus (and in other segments of society) have set up the sexual humiliation of women as a positive value, rewarding it with approval."[12]

Another example of how choice of friends shapes life structure: a young woman senses she is becoming a different person or has a sense she needs to be different, truer to her own humanity than her friends will permit. Eventually she comes to see she never will change if she cannot find friends more appropriate to her emerging sense of herself. When she cannot change her friends' behavior, she can change her friends in the sense of finding new, more appropriate ones.

Daniel Levinson describes the life structure, again, of men, this way:

> By life structure we mean the underlying pattern or design of a person's life at a given time.... A man's life has many components: his occupation, his love relationships, his marriage and family, his relation to himself, his use of solitude, his roles in various social contexts—all the relationships with individuals, groups and institutions that have significance for him. His personality influences and is influenced by his involvement with each of them.... The concept of life structure—the basic pattern or design of a person's life at a given time—gives us a way of looking at the engagement of the individual in society. It requires us to consider both self and world, and the relationships between them.[13]

> How shall we go about describing an analyzing the life structure? The most useful starting point...us to consider the choices a person makes and how he deals with their consequences. The important choices in adult life have to do with work, family, friendships, and love relationships of various kinds, where to live, leisure, involvement in religious, political and community life, immediate and long term goals.[14]

Life structure then says a lot about what we pay attention to. It is found:

...in the check book;

...in a list of the things one has read over the past week or month

...in what one watches on TV or how one watches TV or whether one watches;

...in the tickets one buys and for what;

...in one's phone bill;

...in the kinds of liquids one consumes and under what circumstances;

...in one's credit card bill [and the particular item the charges purchased];

...in one's ways of spending leisure time;

...in the patterns of eating;

...in the mileage of one's commute to work or school;

...in one's patterns of religious practice or lack of it.

My suspicion is that this underlying aspect of our young people's lives has been overlooked in our weekends, and yet these patterned behaviors represent the deepest example of the material conditions of their lives. Will we help them focus more on these actual patterns of living?[15] In a way I have some hesitation in raising this issue for fear it might lead to a renewal of *moralizing* on our weekends. As I understand it, moralizing is a lazy and ineffective form of dealing with human behavior. Rooted in do's and don'ts, it avoids the more difficult but important task of achieving insight through analysis. In the end because life structure arises from choices, young people will have to make their own choices about the patterns of their lives. What we can do is give them the tools for reflecting on these patterns in the light of Jesus' call. They have to decide for themselves, but they don't have to decide by themselves. Will we bring this dimension into our retreats? This is my question.

Of course this is not a question only, or even predominantly, for youth. It is for the entire church, and I myself doubt it can be properly raised for the young unless at the same time this question of life structure is raised also for the wider church. A Methodist church leader raised the question this way:

> To name sin and announce grace is the mission of the church. It's very traditional, and it seems simple to say. But the mainline churches have done a lousy job in naming the suffering of middle-class existence in our time. We haven't told the truth about it. That's the church's greatest sin— not saying that the competitive, driven existence that divides what it is to be a a man or woman, a white or black, is a form of human suffering. It narrows and blocks the human spirit.[16]

She went on to note that U.S. middle class consumerist patterns are killing the persons caught in them, but killing the Third World as well. But most won't be able to recognize the Third World dimension until they see the destruction this life structure is causing in their own lives.

Some Assessments of Youth Weekends at the Present Time

I believe our weekends have great power and greater possibilities, still untapped, though of course the ideas I offer here are adaptable to other sorts of programs, not tied to weekends. In too many youth retreat programs there is a single weekend design, the conversion weekend design. The preparation of team members, recruiting of young people for weekends, planning of schedules, and the follow-up assessment of particular weekends revolve entirely around this single weekend model.

We need additional weekend models to which team members from the conversion weekends and a host of participants who never went on to be team members could be invited. Such weekends might deal with a single issue and then explore ways of responding to it. Of course the weekend itself stands as a significant response to an issue. What might such issues be? Economic inequities/economic justice; homelessness; understanding poverty (the forced poverty of misery and the voluntary poverty of discipleship); peacemaking and justicemaking; The Jesus We Follow: His Times and His Biases; Christian Non-violence; Friendship; Conflict Resolution; Sexual Attraction—Sexual Commitment; Loving God's Earth.

Basically weekends of Christian living for youth are weekends of formation, and they need to be complemented by other, non-weekend, more local formation strategies. I have suggested households of faith or house churches as one such strategy. Here I repeat my lament that the Young Christian Workers, Young Christian Students Movement has not continued in this country. In our country in this century there have always been informal discussion-based movements with great formative power for those in them. Among Roman Catholics I think of the Christian Family Movement that influenced so many adults over a thirty year period. Grassroots communities in Latin America are a striking example of the formative power of such groups. We can experiment to find what groups can meet the needs of our young people. Someone might ask, What is the matter with the local church, the local parish? My answer: In many cases, nothing is the matter with it. However, we should not identify the church entirely with the local parish, which is one form, a very significant one, of the church. We need other forms to realize such a rich reality as the assembly where the Spirit of Jesus is present.

I propose we find ways of experimenting and sharing the outcomes of what we have tried to do. People working with these weekends need a way of networking with others to share these experiments and to foster critical perspectives on their efforts. Possibly people would come together for working sessions, ready to share their ideas on problems identified in advance. If they ever developed such critical working gatherings of those involved in youth weekends could provide much guidance for this important pastoral movement: youth retreats.

Here I have tried to raise some questions about the sort of future we are heading for in our youth retreats or weekend programs. We are, in one way or another, preparing our young people for a future time when problems of discipleship or Christian living will confront them in a vivid way. Obviously we cannot anticipate every difficulty our young people will face and it would be folly to try. Still it is an undeniable fact that what we do in our work the young today will provide them with sound preparation—solid intellectual skills, affective sensitivities, and helpful patterns of behavior—or shoddy preparation. What we do in our work with the young is not innocent. They themselves someday may ask us to answer for the questions we never raised, the problems we—perhaps unwittingly—hid from them, or the proposals for a life worth living we offered them. Let us ponder deeply and have the courage to struggle with these matters, as part of our faith in and for the young and our faith in and for Jesus.

---

[1]Walter Burghardt, "Wedding Three Facets of Justice," *Origins* 20:41 (21 March 1991): 678.

[2]Robert B. Reich, "Secession of the Successful," *The New York Times Magazine* (1/20/91), pp. 16-17; 42-45. It is important to keep in mind that wages are not the same as income. Economist distinguish: wages, household income, personal income, and wealth.

[3]Also in 1988, the first year the new tax code went into effect, taxpayers making over $500,000 per year (0.3% or 3/10 of 1 percent of taxpayers) saved 19.7 billion in taxes, which was 32% of the new code's benefits to all individuals that year. See Henning Gutman, "The Bad News Tax Law," *New York Review of Books* (12 February 1987): 26.

[4]Leonard Silk, "Economic Scene," *The New York Times* (12 May 1989): p. D2.

[5]Barry Bluestone and Bennett Harrison, "The Grim Truth about the Job `Miracle'," *The New York Times* (2/1/87), p. F3.

[6]Editorial, "Home Equity," *Commonweal* (6 May 1988): 259-260.

[7]See, "Towards Democratic Rule of the Church as a Community of God," Chapter 4 of Edward Schillebeeckx, *The Church: The Human Story of God* (New York: Crossroad, 1990), pp. 187-228. Again and again, Schillebeeckx returns to this question of participation in the grassroots reality of the ecclesia.

[8]Ladislaus Orsy, "New Era of Participation in Church Life," *Origins* 17:46 (28 April 1988): 796-800.

[9]David Power, "Households of Faith in the Coming Church," *Worship* 57:3 (1983): 237-255. As radical as Power's essay may seem to some, it is part of a large body of theological thought. See for example, the essays in Edward Schillebeeckx and Johannes Metz, eds., *The Right of the Community to a Priest* (New York: Seabury, 1980), especially those by Derksen, Komonchak, and particularly, the final one, by Schillebeeckx, "The Christian Community and Its Office Bearers," pp. 95-133. See, also, Mary Ann Hinsdale, "Power and Participation in the Church: Voices from the Margins," University of Tulsa, Warren Lecture Series in Catholic Studies, #13, October 1990.

[10]The sources Power cites on the place of poverty in lay-led church renewal from the 11th–14th centuries are worth following up, especially the following: Lester K. Little, *Religious Poverty and the Profit Economy in Medieval Europe* (Ithaca: Cornell U. Press, 1978); David Flood, ed., *Poverty in the Middle Ages* (Werl/Westf.: Diedrich-Coelde, 1975).

[11]Chris O'Sullivan, "Campus Rape Is Usually Fraternity-Related," Letters to the Editor, *The New York Times* (12/5/90), p. A26.

[12]See also, Gerald Eskenazi, "The Male Athlete and Sexual Assault," *The New York Times* 6/3/90, p. L1, L4.

[13]Daniel Levinson, *The Seasons of a Man's Life* (New York: Alfred A. Knopf, 1978), pp. 41-42.

[14]Ibid., p. 43.

[15]See Allan Wheelis, "We Are What We Do," *Commentary* (May 1969): 58-66, esp. 57-58. Later expanded into a small book, this essay is a fine statement of the role of behavior in shaping life. A version of this essay appears in, Kieran Scott and Michael Warren, eds., *Perspectives on Marriage: A Reader* (New York: Oxford University Press, 1993), pp. 217-221.

[16]Mary Hatch, as cited in, Robert N. Bellah, Richard Madsen, William M. Sullivan, Ann Swidler, Steven M. Tipton, *The Good Society* (New York: Alfred A. Knopf, 1991), pp. 210-211.

Chapter 13
Culture, Religion, and Youth

Here I wish to deal with youth in the U.S. in the context, not exclusively of the Christian churches but of any religious group: Jewish, Hindu, Muslim, Buddhist. The problems I describe here go beyond the Christian churches since they are problems of culture, as a system of influences affecting everyone. I will also try to show how religious traditions are also cultures, and how they can and should help the young gain perspective on the wider culture.

One of the great joys of being with the young, either as a parent or a teacher, is seeing latent in them future possibilities of a fuller humanization. I refer to the kind of promise we find in the current behavior of a young person that leads us to suspect or hope this person will make a significant contribution to the lives of others. There grows in this life a capacity for compassion, courage, integrity, humor, or disciplined skill. I meet young people who make me think: in the hands of someone like this human destiny is safe or at least is headed in a good direction. Of course there is another side to these intimations of the future. Sometimes I discern in the young not just the seeds but the flowering shoots of greed, violence, sexual exploitation, and lack of compassion, not human greatness. An intellectually gifted student announces proudly that she has decided to study medicine or the law, two ancient, sometimes noble, professions. I ask why. With the same charm as the announcement, she tells me that that is where the money is. What I am describing here are the possibilities and the obstacles to a flowering of human possibility in the young. These are the concerns of this essay. First however, let me examine the condition of young people in our culture.

Culture as Influencer of Youth

We all recognize that human beings live their social lives together within paradigms, that is, interlocking patterns of thinking and feeling that characterize a particular social system. Ways of looking at reality allow for intersubjectivity, that is the capacity of persons to communicate with and understand each other. People do not so much believe *in* their society's patterns of thought and feeling; they approach life by means of them. To believe in something, that something has to be explicit and

named. No, the paradigms I am referring to here are pre-reflective.
Instead a person views reality and acts *through* the paradigm. A paradigm is the lens through which people see so well that they are unaware
of it as a lens. Edward Farley puts the influence of such paradigms this
way.

> Looked at individually or subjectively the effect of the paradigm on an
> individual is to provide a framework of self-interpretation which reaches
> beyond the lived-space of the individual and beyond the lived-time of his
> or her biographical reach between birth and death. . . . The extension of
> the framework of self-interpretation also reaches beyond the bounds of
> one's own biographical life to include events, persons, even epochs
> which preceded. . .[one's] birth and outcomes which will succeed. . .
> [one's] death.[1]

Of course events can disrupt the paradigm and bring it to awareness, events such as military devastation or economic collapse, or, to a
certain extent, education. But even taking into consideration such paradigm disrupters, it remains true that of all the people in a society the
young tend to absorb the paradigm in a fixed and unquestioning way.
Educators who try to expose for examination aspects of a society's way
of approaching reality know the frustrations of helping the young first
see and then question. When I was a high school teacher concerned
about justice in society, I came to conclude that every two years I was
meeting another group of socially naive persons who systematically
denied my agenda point by point. For them the culture *was the Good
News*, partly because it was the only news they knew. And a suggestion
that there was religious Good News that countered aspects of culture
was bunk.

Every paradigm or way of looking at reality allows not just for common forms of perception but also for common patterns of affectivity and
ways of behaving. Being young in a particular society and culture provide all youth, religious or not, with an experience of life that then can be
reflected on and judged by religious persons. What is the character of the
teen years at the end of the twentieth century and how does it foster a
general structure of feeling? Are there any clues that help us see what life
in the U.S. is like for young people? I would say there are and they signal
the problems affecting the youth of all religious traditions. In Chapters
Six and Seven I have already presented such clues in the form of statistics about suicide and violence. Here I wish to expand some of these
data, as they get at what life is like for young people in the U.S.

The statistical evidence about the cultural climate among the
young is not promising. We have already seen that it suggests that
young people live in an overall climate of violence, showing how success-

fully U.S. society has imprinted in the behavior of the young its ideology of enforcing domination through the use of any and all means, especially, intimidation and violence. To be young in the U.S. means to inhabit fantasies of violence, fears of violence, and actual encounters with violence. Every time I make such a claim in public some leap to deny it. Unfortunately, as powerful and frightening as this claim is, the growing body of statistical evidence grounding it is even more so. What evidence?

The Cultural Climate of Violence

Between 1981 and 1990, the arrest rate for persons under 18 years of age for murder increased 60.1%; for forcible rape, it increased 28.2%; for aggravated assault, it increased 56.5%; for motor vehicle theft, it increased 72.6%; for weapons possession, it increased 41.2%.[2] Using the Crime Index, which includes two related categories of criminal acts: *violent crimes* of murder, forcible rape, robbery and aggravated assault and *property crimes* of burglary, larceny-theft, motor vehicle theft and arson, in 1990 persons under 18 were 28% of all those arrested for such crimes; persons under 21 were 43% of all arrested; persons under 25 were 57% of all arrested.[3] Further in the U.S. today more teenage boys die of gunshot wounds than all natural causes put together.[4]

These figures carry forward a pattern noted in the U.S. beginning about 1950. I have already pointed out that between 1960 and 1972 the number of females under 18 arrested for violent crimes rose 388%, while the rate for similar males went up 203%[5]. Between 1981 and 1990, arrests of women under 18 for aggravated assault increased 79.1%. In New York City, arrests of youth under the age of sixteen for robbery increased 100% in the six-year period, 1985-1991; for assault, they increased over 200% in the same period; for possession of a loaded gun they increased over 500% in those years.[6] To extend this tale of woe a bit, the FBI reported in 1985 that youth aged 15 and younger had committed 381 murders and non-negligent manslaughter; over 18,000 aggravated assaults, almost 14,000 robberies and 2,645 rapes. Between 1978 and 1983, the fastest-growing areas in juvenile crime were among the youngest groups: 13, 12, 11 and 10.[7] During those years, the rate of referrals to juvenile courts rose 38% for 12-year-olds; 37% for 13-year-olds, 22% for 12-year-olds, and 15% for 10-year-olds, the youngest age for which such statistics were available.

Sexual Violence

Sexual violence among even young teens deserves special attention from those examining the structure of feeling among young people.

Rape and other forms of sexual abuse now form a pattern in our society across the socio-economic spectrum. Rape is not a crime of lust but one of violence, in which the dignity of another is violated. A 1985 *New York Times* report on date rape noted that the preliminary data of a three-year survey of 6,500 students in 35 universities found that one of every eight women surveyed said she had been raped, most often by someone she dated. A 1987 study of 6, 150 women students at 32 U.S. colleges found that 27.5 % of college women reported having been raped at some point since the age of 14.[8] Neil Malamuth's survey of 2,000 college men found that 35% said they might rape a women if they knew they would not be caught.[9] When Malamuth replicated his study but changed "rape" to "force a woman to have sex," 50% of the men surveyed said "they might."[10] These attitudes among men do not begin after age nineteen but emerge form a pattern of thinking that begins much earlier. The National Center for Juvenile Justice reports that from 1976 to 1986, the arrest rate for 13 and 14 year olds on rape charges went from 20 per 100,000 children to 40. Professionals treating sexual offenders now find they enter treatment programs at thirteen, ten and even eight years of age.[11]

Cultural Coding in the Young

Where does this behavior come from? How does it increase and how does it come to affect ever younger groups of young people? Here I will use two angles for answering these questions: the notion of "cultural coding" and the related matter of the "orchestration of attention." I first came across cultural coding in an essay of theologian Thomas Berry. Since we are coded to think and feel as our culture deems we should, we tend to see only what the cultural coding of the scientific-technological age permits us to see. Berry says "cultural coding, like genetic coding, establishes values and patterns of action. Especially in cultural coding the demonic depends on what might be called an altered state of consciousness, a trance state."[12] We accept as normal demonic systems of evil, even when these in fact represent a kind of social madness. The demonic trance state of course tends to be unquestioned and will not be re-cast easily.

For example, violence has been so successfully encoded in our young people they consider it as a normal state of affairs. Young men and women gather for fun and refreshment—let's say on weekends—at places where commonly they see people punched, kicked, or knocked down. This kind of physical violence is so common they do not even comment on it when recounting their time in these places. They observe vicious forms of verbal violence and take them so much for granted they cannot be reflected on or questioned. Ask young women about the physical abuse some of their friends receive from their boyfriends, a matter they rarely bring up in casual conversation or even in class sessions on conflict, and you may find out that the cultural coding is there unexplored and unexamined.

For Berry the restoration of a true sense the human can take place only in a "confrontation with the demonic aspect of our existing mode of cultural coding" out of which can emerge a new coding.[13] The work of re-coding, I am saying, is a work needing much more explicit focus in all religious groups, and especially in their work with youth. In the churches we can have our young people chirping merrily away in our group-singing sessions and can be pleased with our own ability to get them into the swing of things—without ever dealing with the coding of violence they carried into the room with them. Berry uses the word "confrontation" to speak of re-coding. This is an important word, because re-coding cannot be done without some kind of radical confrontation with the existing code. That code must be surfaced, named, and then contested before an alternate code can be proposed. I want to call christian youth ministry to the importance of this work of confrontation for the Christic humanization of the young.

Culture's Orchestration of Attention

In probing more deeply where the violence cited above comes from I suggest those who love the young might pay more attention to what the young pay attention to. What we pay attention to shapes our human spirits. The orchestration of attention in our day is a special problem for religious traditions, since they offer distinctive ways of paying attention to the world. Here is what one social commentator has said recently about this problem of attention today.

> One of the most profitable commodities in the modern world is human attention. Whoever can harvest it in wholesale quantities can make money in kind. In the United States, one Nielsen rating point reflects 1 percent of the country's 90 million television households. One percentage point for a network in prime-time audience share represents more than $30 million in added revenues each year. Nothing in human experience has prepared men, women, and children for the modern television techniques of fixing human attention and creating the uncritical mood required to sell goods, many of which are marginal at best to human needs.[14]

Those who harvest human attention via television also focus that attention on numberless depictions of human behavior in acted-out narratives. Such narratives imagine the world for those who see them.

Who imagines the world for the young and who tells them the stories? How is that world imagined and what is that story? These are two significant questions for those concerned with the human possibilities of the young. Scenarios of the successful use of dominative force abound in film and TV. Perhaps the most powerful of such scenario has not been actually enacted but has been persistently announced for years in the rhetoric of mutually assured destruction.[15] Scenarios of self-destructive vehicle abuse (cars, trucks, motorcycles, aircraft) are common in films made for the teen market. As for sexual violence, in 1982, one in twenty commercially released films depicted violent acts against women. In 1983, the rate was one in eight depicting such acts.[16] Feminists have long pointed out how many films depict a woman alone as a victim of violence. It takes time to convince young people of the significance of this fact. Some are quick to say that such a message is good because it warns women to be careful. They are not so quick to assess what this fear of not-so-latent violence does to the spirits of women. They are much slower to see the significance for men of a continual message that *a woman alone is a potential victim, almost always of a male.*

Someone might point out that these statistics give evidence, not so much of violence among the young, but of how relatively low is its incidence. Cross-cultural comparisons make the importance of the evidence clearer. For example, between 1980 and 84, the incidence of rape in the U.S. remained stable at 36 per 100,000 [an extremely low estimate], but in Western Europe it remained stable at 4.8 per 100,000. In Canada, Australia and New Zealand, in those years rape had risen from 10.5 to 14.1.[17] Apparently there are social and cultural climates that make these acts more possible in one social setting than in another. The significance of statistics is always as a pointer to behavior more prevalent than the statistics themselves. In the end, the alarming aspect of the culture of violence in which young people in the U.S. live is that the young themselves are haunted by fantasies of violence, with themselves as either victims or victimizers, at the same time they tend to be unaware of these very fantasies. Many young women have grown up taking for granted as part of normal life the sense of danger imprinted on their consciousness by being told in various ways that unless a woman takes special cautions, she will become a victim.

What I have been pointing out here is how effective—notice I do not say inevitable—is the cultural coding of the young. The conditions for the cultural colonization of the young have always been in place in all societies. The conditions for the widespread cultural colonization of the time and attention of the young through vivid electronic narratives imagining for them the purposes and possibilities of human existence, those conditions have been in place scarcely forty years. As one social critic puts it:

> [I]n the last half of the twentieth century, the degree to which mass audience culture has colonized the social space available to the ordinary person for reading, discussions, and critical thought must be counted as the major event of social history in our time. Television, film, and photography, far from making culture democratic, have fostered the wide dissemination of industrialized entertainment so that the capacity of persons to produce their own culture in the widest meaning of the term has become restricted.[18]

The word "colonize" might well signal deep alarm among those with religious sensitivities, let alone religious commitments. What is being colonized are the spirits of persons we all know. Stanley Aronowitz is not alone in using this language of colonization. In writing of what she calls "the fashionable mind," Kennedy Fraser, whom I have already quoted more than once, writes that "...fashion is now setting out boldly to colonize the world's mysterious islands of individuality and the hitherto unexplored territory of the inner life."[19]

These descriptions of the subjugation of the spirits of many in our time are disheartening. Yet, I believe there are counter-conditions for the cultural liberation of the young by means of a vivid living out of a particular religious imagination: of the Muslim, Christian, Jewish, Hindu, Buddhist, and so forth. However, I fear those counter-conditions are far too little in place. To that matter I now turn my attention by asking first, What is culture?

What Is Culture?

The description of culture I find most useful is the one the late British scholar, Raymond Williams, offers in his book, *The Sociology of Culture*. What is useful about Williams' approach to culture is that it gives us a way of thinking about and examining the processes by which a culture is produced and thus de-mystifies the obscure notion of culture held by many people. Williams describes culture as "*a signifying system* [emphasis his] through which...a social order is communicated, reproduced, experienced, and explored."[20]

Every social order needs a signifying system to communicate its inner core in various modes: in conceptual categories but also in non-logical symbols, such as images, heroes and heroines, rituals and narratives. The signifying system sets forth a particular social order's story of reality, that it, its imagination of what the human project is all about. Especially helpful about this description is that it describes any of the many religious traditions. They represent, each in a distinctive way, a social order with its own symbols, rituals, heroes and heroines, and with its own imagination of the purpose of the human project. My specific interest here is not in each tradition as a global phenomenon but in its local embodiment in particular communities: temple, synagogue, mosque or church.

We who embrace religious traditions dwell then in two cultures, one the wider social culture of our nation and its economic system, the other, the narrower religious one that exists within the wider "secular" culture. An important difference separates these two cultures. The narrower, religious one makes a bold and overt claim that *its* meanings are ultimate and hold a decisive place in directing the behavior of those embracing these meanings. Since the religious culture's meanings are prior, they relativize the claims of other social orders and signifying systems.

This rendition sounds compact and neat until we realize that the wider culture also claims that its meanings are ultimate, but rarely does so explicitly. The wider culture's claim is implicit and made quietly made as an assumption about reality. Ironically, the implicit claim can be more powerful than the explicit one. Hard enough to counter a claim not clearly made; harder still is challenging a claim not admitted to exist.

A Religious Tradition's Relation to the Wider Culture

As a signifying system by which a social order is communicated, a religious tradition, as least usually, is not against the wider culture. Standing squarely within that wider culture, it welcomes and applauds every feature fostering the authentic humanization of persons. Because it embraces a religious imagination of human possibilities, any local embodiment of a religious tradition rejoices in the ways social systems promote the human project. However, a particular local gathering within a religious tradition is clearly a zone of judgment, assessing both the social order and its signifying system by the criteria of the tradition's vision of the dignity of persons. A proper formula for the way these assessments are made might be: Quick to affirm what enriches the human project but unafraid to point out what diminishes it.

Actually a tradition carries within it vestiges of the positive features of the many cultures within which it has existed. Its music, its rituals, its dogmatic formulations, its forms of communication, and its polities have been influenced by centuries of embracing what was truly humanizing in the various cultures it met. This positive influence on religious traditions still continues in varied ways, such as the application of say, management science to the coordination of the tradition's human resources. What I am saying is that, yes, the tradition exists within the wider culture but also that the wider exists to an extent within the tradition—and it is here that I have to add, "And not always in positive ways." Patriarchy, sexism, homophobia, polities that operate out of domination-subordination thinking—vestiges of these inhumanities can continue to infect any tradition. Yet, however much this fact is true, there is another side to every religious tradition. A religion, claiming its meanings are ultimate and transcendent, also offers a standpoint from which to question and judge the wider culture.

Religious Traditions as Zones of Judgment

The religious tradition as a zone of judgment functions in two ways. It judges the wider culture at the same time it itself is judged by its own religious texts and tradition. These texts constantly bring the tradition in its local, regional and international embodiments before the bar of its own criteria. Embedded in many of the texts themselves are examples showing the texts themselves arose out of this kind of inner judgment. Judgment is an indispensable feature of any religious tradition.

Here, I want to make a most important point about the salvific or liberating role of religious traditions in the U.S. We live in a time when fewer and fewer places of free public assembly are being used by our people for discourse about the course of our national policies. Union halls used to be such places, but they are in a state of decline; political clubs used to be such places, but they too are in decline in a time of reduced political activism. Predictions are that even movie theaters, now among the few common places of assembly left, will be out of existence within thirty years. That leaves two de-politicized zones of assembly: the chief one, the shopping mall; the second one, the sports assembly. In this kind of society, the local assembly points of religious traditions: mosques, temples, churches, and synagogues remain important and potentially powerful zones from which the policies and procedures of the dominant culture can be questioned and contested from an alternative standpoint. If I wanted to control a society's overall agenda and to orchestrate it towards greater selfishness and greater domination over others, I would be very concerned about people assembling in local groups around religious values. They represent a zone of judgment, evaluating social reality from transcendent perspectives.

Youth and Culture

There are no youth problems that are not in fact human problems found among all age groups but now come to roost among the young. With the prevalence of electronic communications, especially electronic story-telling, everyone, including youth, has unlimited access to compelling, acted-out versions of reality. Especially through television everyone has access to vivid imaginations of what life is all about. In consumerist capitalism, many of these imaginations are part of a strategy for orchestrating consumption. They are paid for by commercial interests. They are shown in a context that stresses the centrality of having, and often enough the stories themselves involve dramatizations of good and evil, with the good being the good of having and the evil being that of having one's goods snatched away.

Here we have a world of signification being packaged for people. It is not the culture of the people but the culture concocted for the consumption of the people. The main kind of agency envisaged for people is to watch someone's else's story and then buy the products behind it. To some extent, thus far not fully assessed, electronic communications tend to diminish cultural agency among many people, in the sense they tend to be living in someone else's world of meaning and tend to be passive or mute when it comes to articulating their own world of meaning.

How do religious meanings fare in such a cultural climate? In answering, one principle must by kept clear: Religious meanings are not self-maintaining. Because the meanings of a religion represent realities not easily evident, those meanings need to be worked at actively if they are to retain their hold on our imaginations. Religious meanings cannot be maintained without cultural agency on the part of all those involved. This fact actually is what is behind the idea that regular participation at worship is a potentially important part of religious living. Without gathering with a chorus of others who hold these meanings in common, the meanings themselves can come to seem illusory.

Religious traditions have used many procedures to maintain their religious meanings. All of them are forms of cultural agency, calling people to work with and on the meanings that bind the faithful together. The basic procedure called for in a time of increasing cultural passivity is dialogue towards living out the meanings in specific forms of practice. Dialogue is an authentic and key form of any cultural agency but *the seminal form* of religious cultural agency. As a grappling with the religious zone of signification and with the religious problematic, dialogue lays the groundwork for testing the truth claims of a religion by the acid test of practice.

Speaking now as a Christian, I find unfortunately that too many of the churches ape society's way of dealing with the young. They expect the young to be consumers of the meaning-system supposedly lived out by the church. Today, however an important theological principle being recovered world-wide, especially by means of liberation theology, is that all persons have a right, indeed a human duty, to become co-producers of religious meaning. This principle has yet to be applied widely to young people in local churches, indeed, in some places, to lay people in general. As far as I can determine, the youth ministry efforts that in fact are influencing young people toward discipleship do so because they allow the young to become co-producers of the religious culture in which they stand. And the efforts that are failing are those that reduce young people to the status of consumers, demanding they accept doctrinal capital on a "handout" basis and then expecting them to put it to good use, i.e., "invest it" in living practice.

Such a process is quite different from laying open to them the community's resources and inviting them to use them for engaging in the production of meaning: through dialogue, through struggling with the problematic of today's world, through allowing the keen questioning of assumptions, including doctrinal ones, found among many young people, and especially through action for justice. By participating actively in this religious culture as a co-producer, a person truly enters it as a zone of judgment exposing what is unacceptable in the wider culture. Speaking of liberating education in general, Aronowitz makes a point similar to my own here.

> [T]he capacity of humans to gain critical perspective upon their social world can no longer to be taken for granted. The restricted language and thought codes produced by the reduction of all thought to its technical dimensions reach far into the culture, encompassing schools as well as communications, the public as well as the private spheres of discourse.... The issue is the capacity for theoretical or conceptual thought itself. When people lack such competence, social action that transcends the struggle for justice within the empirically given rules of social organization and discourse is impossible.[21]

Participation in the life of the community within a religious tradition means participation in the ongoing creation of the culture of that tradition, in the sense that one comes to an authentic, and very possibly an original, word about its religious quest in our time. But nobody participates in the creation of culture without participation in the creation or re-forming of the polity of that culture. To have a say in the production of the culture of the tradition means likewise having to some extent a say in the way its power is used.

To repeat this point: I suspect the stumbling block to the full participation of youth in many religious traditions is that they are invited to participate in the *reproduction* of religious meaning but not in the true, original production of that meaning. At least such is my view of what is happening in the Roman Catholic Church with its special stumbling block to women, who because of gender are deemed permanently lay and to youth, who because of age are exclusively lay.

In a time when electronic communications invite us to the "illusory participative," that is, to enter the slick and easily entertaining visions of life absorbed from the electronic dream machines, religious traditions have a powerful antidote if it will invite its people including the young, to enter an alternative world of meaning enriched by a deeper human imagination than that of the consumerist society. In my understanding, all religious traditions embrace the poor and society's victims as living temples of God. These victims call religious people to enter also a zone of judgment, using the lens of God's ways as a basic way of seeing the world. When the young become part of such communities of religious judgment, all reality is potentially changed, suffused with God's goodness and with new possibilities of human response.

---

[1]Edward Farley, *Ecclesial Reflection: An Anatomy of Theological Method* (Philadelphia: Fortress, 1982), p. 360.

[2]U.S. Justice Department, *Uniform Crime Reports for the United States, 1990* (August 1991), p. 178.

[3]Ibid., p. 174.

[4]U.S. Catholic Bishops' Statement, "Putting Children and Families First: A Challenge for Our Church, Nation and World," *Origins* 21:25 (28 November 1991): p. 395.

[5]These last figures are from, Edward Wynne, "Adolescent Alienation and Youth Policy," *Teacher College Record* 78:1 (1976): 23-40.

[6]Joseph B. Treaster & Mary B.W. Tabor, "Teen-age Gunslinging Rises, Seeking Protection and Profit," *The New York Times* (12 February 1992): Pp. A 1, B 6.

[7]Peter Applebome, "Juvenile Crime: The offenders are Younger and the Offenses More Serious," *The New York Times* (3 February 1987), p. A 16.

[8]Mary P. Koss, Gidycz and Wisniewski, The Scope of Rape: Incidence and Prevalence of Sexual Aggression and Victimization, *Journal of Consulting and Clinical Psychology* 55:2 (1987): 162-170.

[9]Beth Sherman, "A New Recognition of the Realities of 'Date Rape'," *The New York Times* (23 october 1985), pp. C1, C14.

[10]See, Neil Malamuth, "The Attraction to Sexual Aggression Scale: Part One," *The Journal of Sex Research* 26:1 (February 1989): 26-49, at 37.

[11]Felicity Barringer, "Children as Sexual Prey, and Predators," *The New York Times* (5 May 1989): P. A1, A16. See also the following: the special issue of *Sojourners*, November 1984 on this matter; the September 1980 number of *Cosmopolitan*, where results of a survey of 106,000 women found that 24% claimed to have been raped, 51% by "friends"; "Results of Ms. Study," [of rape] Ms. October 1985, p. 58.

¹²Thomas Berry, "Classical Western Spirituality and the American Experience," *Cross Currents* 31:4 (1981-82): 388-399, at 396.

¹³Ibid., p. 399. Berry's concern in this essay is not with the cultural coding of the young but with a wider and even more important question of the relation of the earth to the human. I have taken his ideas out of context and applied them to the problem of the cultural coding of the young.

¹⁴Ben H. Bagdikian, "The Lords of the Global Village," *The Nation* (12 June 1989): 805-820, at 819.

¹⁵See Chapter 7, pp. 80-90.

¹⁶Daniel Goleman, "Violence against Women in Films," *The New York Times* (28 August 1984), pp. C1, C5. The research reported in this article is quite important and worth following up. Almost a third of men who watched films of extreme violence against women found themselves sexually stimulated by those acts. Researchers also found that repeated viewings of such films made them progressively less upsetting, more enjoyable, and less debasing to women. The men who viewed such material in the study were also more likely to find the victim at fault for what happened.

¹⁷*The New York Times* (4 May 1988), p. A15. Keep in mind, though, that substantive research has now been done on how under-reported rape is in the U.S. See, Mary P. Koss, et al., "The Scope of Rape: Incidence and Prevalence of Sexual Aggression in a National Sample of Higher Education Students," *Journal of Consulting and Clinical Psychology* 55:2 (1987): 163-170.

¹⁸Stanley Aronowitz and Henry Giroux, *Education Under Siege* (Mass: Bergin and Garvey, 1985), p. 51. My assumption is that his passage was written by Aronowitz.

¹⁹Kennedy Fraser, *The Fashionable Mind: Reflections on Fashion, 1970-82* (Boston: David R. Godine, 1984), p. 150.

²⁰Raymond Williams, *The Sociology of Culture* (New York: Schocken Books, 1982), p. 13.

²¹Aronowitz and Giroux, *Education Under Siege,* p. 47.